**THE COUNCIL OF BI**

D1047580

HOW TO PROTECT YOUR BUSINESS

Published with the

 COUNCIL OF BETTER BUSINESS BUREAUS

by The Benjamin **B** Company, Inc.

in association with **PRENTICE HALL**
Englewood Cliffs, NJ
07632

TO GET ADDITIONAL COPIES

Single copies of this book are available from your local bookstore, local Better Business Bureau (see Appendix B), or the Council of Better Business Bureaus, 4200 Wilson Boulevard, Arlington, VA 22203.

Special discounts for bulk quantities are offered to business firms, associations, government agencies, and other organizations that plan to use this book as a promotional, educational, or public relations tool. For orders up to 500 copies, contact Prentice Hall - Business Information and Publishing Division, Englewood Cliffs, NJ 07632.

Back cover identification and message are available, subject to CBBB approval, on special printing orders. Contact the publisher, The Benjamin Company, 21 Dupont Avenue, White Plains, NY 10605.

Research and Writing: Virginia Schomp, Neil W. Sandler
Project Director and Editor: Roger F. Campbell, Jr.
Editorial Assistants: Rosann Catania, Anne Erena (Benjamin), Ilana Brilliant (CBBB)
Designer: Pam Forde Graphics
Typographer: Graphic Circle Inc.

ISBN: 0-13-430521-3 Trade paperback, Prentice Hall Edition
      0-87502-244-8 Trade paperback, Benjamin Company edition
      0-87502-245-6 Mass market paperback, Benjamin Company edition

Library of Congress Cataloging-in-Publication Data
Schomp, Virginia.
  How to protect your business from fraud, scams & crime / (research and writing,
  Virginia Schomp, Neil W. Sandler). — 2nd ed. p. cm.
  At head of title: The Council of Better Business Bureaus.
  Rev. ed. of: How to protect your business / Neil W. Sandler. 1985.
  Includes index.
  ISBN 0-87502-244-8 (pbk.): $14.95. — ISBN 0-87502-245-6 (mass market pbk.): $5.95.—
  ISBN 0-13-430521-3 (trade pbk.): $14.95
  1. Commercial crimes — United States — Prevention. 2. White collar crimes —
  United States — Prevention. I. Sandler, Neil W. II. Sandler, Neil W. How to
  protect your business. III. Council of Better Business Bureaus. IV. Title
  HV6769. S27 1992
  658.4'73 — dc20   91-34385
                                                                    CIP

Produced and published by The Benjamin Company, Inc.
                           21 Dupont Avenue
                           White Plains, NY 10605

94 93 92 91   10 9 8 7 6 5 4 3 2 1

*This book is dedicated to helping
the American business community
fight those crimes that needlessly raise
the costs of goods and services
to its customers.*

Contents

Foreword   9
Preface   10
Acknowledgments   11
Introduction   12

One of the fastest growing, most lucrative industries in the U.S. is crime against business. In the 1990s, illegal proceeds will exceed revenues earned in high-tech fields such as aerospace technology, computers, and bioengineering. While crime against business has driven many companies out of business, an alert and educated businessperson is not defenseless.

The BBB Works with Business
You Are Not Defenseless
Figuratively Speaking
The Role of the BBB
How You Can Help

SECTION I

SCHEMES AGAINST BUSINESS

CHAPTER 1   **Office Supply Schemes and "Paper Pirates"** 19

This multimillion-dollar-a-year scheme involves the unethical but often legal sale of poor-quality, off-brand office supplies to businesses that think they are getting a name brand product at a special discount price.

The Case of the Careless Copier
Unethical But Legal Sales Pitches
"WATS-line Hustlers"
How to Protect Your Business
What to Do If You Are Victimized

CHAPTER 2   **Phony Invoice Schemes** 27

Billing schemes typically prey on the inefficiency of business. Most cases involve the mailing of phony invoices to employees who are not careful enough in scrutinizing bills being processed for payment. Includes section on directory advertising fraud.

The Case of the Bogus Bill
Anatomy of a Scam
Bogus Yellow Pages Bills
How to Protect Your Business
What to Do If You Are Victimized

CHAPTER 3   **Charitable Solicitation Schemes**   37

American businesses are contacted regularly for donations to charities, foundations, and other worthy causes. Unfortunately, each year millions of dollars targeted toward worthy purposes are diverted into the pockets of swindlers.

The Case of the Uninformed Donor
Corporate Contributions to Charity
How to Protect Your Business
What to Do If You Are Victimized

CHAPTER 4   **Loan Broker Frauds and
                    "Advance Fee" Schemes**   51

While most organizations that lend money to businesses are legitimate, some self-proclaimed "loan brokers" offer to lend money they cannot provide – then abscond with the so-called "advance fees."

The Case of the Vanishing Broker
How Legitimate Loan Brokers Work
Sorry, Wrong Number
How to Protect Your Business
What to Do If You Are Victimized

CHAPTER 5   **Bankruptcy Fraud**   59

Taking advantage of provisions in the federal bankruptcy codes that are aimed at helping those with failed businesses get back on their feet, con artists and some formerly honest businesspeople are making a living by intentionally running businesses into the ground for profit.

The Case of the Menacing Merchants
How Bankruptcy Fraud Works
A Variety of Schemes
How to Protect Your Business
What to Do If You Are Victimized

CHAPTER 6   **Business Opportunity
                    and Investment Schemes**   65

"Once-in-a-lifetime" opportunities to invest in a business in which you are all but guaranteed to convert your investment of several thousand dollars into many times that amount are rare at best. In most cases, the only thing that really is guaranteed is a con artist willing and able to rid you of your investment capital.

The Case of Bitter Sweets
Business Opportunities Abound
Inside the Schemes
How to Protect Your Business
What to Do If You Are Victimized

CHAPTER 7   **Telemarketing Crimes**   79

Many schemes, scams, and frauds are perpetrated by phone, with these illegal spin-offs of the fast-growing telemarketing industry netting the "telescammers" billions of dollars each year.

The Case of the Vanishing Vendor
Typical Telemarketing Scams
How to Protect Your Business
What to Do If You Are Victimized

SECTION II

EXTERNAL CRIME

CHAPTER 8   **Product Counterfeiting**   95

Clothing designers aren't the only ones who earn a living by selling their name brand fashions. Unscrupulous manufacturers of clothing and other goods produce cheap imitations, then sell the low-quality merchandise to unwitting consumers as the real thing. Both the original manufacturers and consumers lose out.

The Case of the Buyer's Blues
An Epidemic of Fraud: From High Fashion to High Tech
Intellectual Property Rights
How to Protect Your Business
What to Do If You Are Victimized

CHAPTER 9   **Crimes Practiced on Cashiers**   103

Quick-change artists, who confuse cashiers and walk away with more change than they originally paid, have been succeeded by more sophisticated schemers. The quick-change scheme is now joined by price tag and container switches and refund fraud, among others. Includes special section on counterfeit currency.

The Case of the Sticky Tickets
Cashier Rip-offs: A Retailer's Nightmare
How to Protect Your Business
What to Do If You Are Victimized

CHAPTER 10   **Shoplifting**   115

Professional and nonprofessional shoplifters have been known to steal just about any item for sale in a store. Keeping employees and managers alert for these culprits represents the first line of defense.

A Case of Sticky Fingers
Shoplifter Profiles
How to Protect Your Business
What to Do If You Are Victimized

CHAPTER 11   **Credit Card Fraud**   125

As the use of credit cards almost replaces the use of cash for many Americans, great new horizons are drawn for criminals who find new ways to tap into this vast interchange of money. While stolen cards remain the primary avenue of crime, other schemes are on the rise.

The Case of the Card Crook
The Credit Card Revolution
Profiles of Credit Card Fraud
Credit Card Laundering
How to Protect Your Business
What to Do If You Are Victimized

CHAPTER 12   **Check Fraud**   133

"Bounced" checks written against insufficient funds remain the most common problem, but businesses also must be alert to a variety of check fraud schemes.

> *The Case of the Friendly Forger*
> *Types of Bad Checks*
> *How to Protect Your Business*
> *What to Do If You Are Victimized*

CHAPTER 13   **Coupon Fraud**   147

Coupons offering "cents off" on everyday consumer necessities and appearing in magazines, newspapers, and the mail represent a $3.5-billion-a-year business that is the target of coupon fraud schemes.

> *The Case of the Free Lunch*
> *Couponing: a $3.5-Billion Business*
> *How Couponing and Coupon Fraud Work*
> *How to Protect Your Business*
> *What to Do If You Are Victimized*

CHAPTER 14   **Cargo Theft**   153

Unauthorized shipments, overshipments, short packaging, night thefts from trucks, and tailgate thefts in broad daylight are just a few of the ways honest businesses suffer heavy losses at the hands of dishonest employees, customers, or bandits.

> *The Case of the Wheeler-Dealers*
> *Cargo Theft: Ten-billion-dollar Annual Losses*
> *How to Protect Your Business*
> *What to Do If You Are Victimized*

CHAPTER 15   **Industrial Espionage**   159

Corporate information theft by industrial spies and disgruntled employees costs American businesses billions annually in missed sales and wasted research and development costs.

> *The Case of the Suspect Supervisor*
> *Corporate Gold Miners*
> *Information Seekers Abroad*
> *How to Protect Your Business*
> *What to Do If You Are Victimized*

SECTION III

INTERNAL CRIME

CHAPTER 16   **Pilferage and Embezzlement**   171

Company books altered so that stolen funds or goods cannot be tracked easily, employees who pocket customers' cash, items eaten directly from the shelves of a grocery store – all fall into this diverse and highly damaging category. But there are prevention strategies.

> *The Case of the Cooked Books*
> *Crimes of Confidence*
> *How to Protect Your Business*
> *What to Do If You Are Victimized*

CONTENTS

CHAPTER 17 **Bribery, Kickbacks, and Payoffs** 181

Unethical and illegal payments of money, goods, and services occur at all levels of business and government. The answers to a series of questions can help you spot suspicious activities.

The Case of the Collusive Consultant
Behind the Schemes
Two Types of Schemes
How to Protect Your Business
What to Do If You Are Victimized

CHAPTER 18 **Insurance Fraud** 187

While the majority of insurance fraud cases harm insurance companies, many are carried out against businesses that insure with nonexistent or "paper" insurance companies.

The Case of the Crooked Claimant
Common Types of Insurance Fraud
How to Protect Your Business
Insurance Companies Fight Back
What to Do If You Are Victimized

CHAPTER 19 **Computer Crime** 195

Computer crimes provide sophisticated criminals and "hackers" with a "window into the system" through which they can manipulate information or steal funds. Considering that this is the Information Age, thefts of information can prove costly.

The Case of the Systematic Stickup
Computer Vulnerability: Easy Access to Business Data
Typical Computer Crimes
Desktop Forgery
How to Protect Your Business
What to Do If You Are Victimized

APPENDIX A 207

A list of government agencies and associations that businesses can contact for advice and assistance. Includes addresses, phone numbers, and areas of activity.

APPENDIX B 211

Directory of the local Better Business Bureaus in the U.S. and Canada, including addresses and phone numbers.

GLOSSARY OF TERMS 216

INDEX 222

Foreword

The Better Business Bureau for decades has been synonymous with integrity and fair dealing in the business community. In today's business world of instant information through world-wide computer networks, maintaining integrity and solvency is a greater challenge than ever before.

I was pleased to learn that the Council of Better Business Bureaus had revised its handbook on protecting businesses from frauds and criminal activities. The largest corporations generally have the skills and personnel to protect themselves or to bring legal action when necessary. But small business owners must guard as much against the potential financial disaster of rip-off artists, scams, and misrepresentations as they do against the common shoplifter.

As a former small business owner before coming to the Senate, I can think of many times the information in the Council's handbook would have saved me money and embarrassment.

This comprehensive guidebook contains a wealth of useful information and reminds us that knowledge is still the best defense.

Dale Bumpers

Senator Dale Bumpers, (D-Ark.)
Chairman
Senate Small Business Committee

Preface

New schemes and scams, as well as variations on old frauds, cost U.S. businesses billions of dollars each year. Inevitably, this loss is passed on to consumers in the form of higher prices for goods and services.

Concerned about the ever-increasing menace of defrauders who prey upon unwary merchants and their employees, the Council of Better Business Bureaus has revised this authoritative guidebook *How To Protect Your Business,* which informs and educates proprietors about possible external and internal crimes against their establishments.

In revising the book, we contacted scores of government agencies and trade groups and relied upon our extensive experience as reported by the Better Business Bureau system nationwide. These sources provided new information on the latest scams against businesses, including telemarketing crimes, industrial espionage, fax directory schemes, credit card laundering, phony yellow pages solicitations, and medical insurance scams.

Recognizing that knowledge and awareness on the part of businesses is the best deterrent to these illegal activities, we believe this comprehensive guidebook will help in preventing such practices, and serve as a constructive tool for upholding the principles of honesty and fairness in the workplace and marketplace.

James H. McIlhenny
President
Council of Better Business Bureaus

Acknowledgments

Many individuals representing public and private agencies, organizations, and corporations contributed time and effort to this project. We gratefully acknowledge their assistance – the information they provided, their comments, criticisms, and suggestions. Their names are too numerous to mention, but special thanks must go to our friends at:

Alliance Against Fraud in Telemarketing
American Association of Fund-Raising Counsel
American Bankers Association
American Insurance Association
American Society for Industrial Security
Audit Bureau of Circulations
Bureau of the Census
Commodity Futures Trading Commission
Direct Marketing Association
Dun & Bradstreet Corporation
Faulkner & Gray
Federal Bureau of Investigation
Federal Trade Commission
Internal Revenue Service
International Anticounterfeiting Coalition
International Franchise Association
Marketing Logistics
MasterCard
MCI Communications Corporation
National Association of Credit Card Merchants
National Cargo Security Council
National Fire Protection Association
National Office Products Association
National Retail Federation
NCH Promotional Services
U.S. Attorney General's Office
U.S. Chamber of Commerce
U.S. Commissioner of Patents and Trademarks
U.S. Customs Service
U.S. Department of Commerce
U.S. Department of Justice
U.S. General Accounting Office
U.S. Postal Service
U.S. Secret Service
U.S. Small Business Administration

Introduction

One of the fastest-growing, most lucrative industries in America today is crime against business.

In the 1990s, the dollar value of cash, merchandise, and information obtained through employee theft, computer fraud, office supply schemes, bribes, kickbacks, credit card fraud, and related crimes will far outpace the value legitimately earned in high-tech industries such as aerospace, computers, and bio-engineering. Surprisingly, knowledgeable crime watchers predict that for the most part this accelerating crime wave will not comprise such familiar, well-publicized phenomena as burglary and street crime but rather white-collar crimes and a whole new class of schemes and frauds perpetrated both within and outside targeted businesses.

Consider the following facts:

- Losses due to product counterfeiting have been estimated at more than $2 billion annually for the U.S. computer industry, $5 billion for pharmaceutical companies, and $3 billion to $6 billion a year for the U.S. chemical industry, according to industry sources.

- Approximately one-fifth of the investigative staff of the Federal Bureau of Investigation (FBI) in 1989 was targeted exclusively at detecting white-collar crime. The result: over 4,000 convictions and an estimated $1.5 billion in potential economic losses prevented.

- A retail theft is committed every five seconds, reports the Small Business Administration, with these thefts costing each American $150 a year.

- The National Office Products Association cites annual losses of $50 million to businesses due to office supply schemes, but notes the actual figure may be even higher.

- One major credit card company reports losses due to the fraudulent use of cards nearly doubled in just one year – from $151 million in 1989 to $300 million in 1990.
- Computer crimes perpetrated in a scant 0.0003 second 3 milliseconds) have netted these specialized criminals millions of dollars.
- Property and casualty insurance fraud results in annual losses of an estimated $20 billion, according to the American Insurance Association.
- White-collar crime is responsible for the loss of billions of dollars annually to government, business, and citizens nationwide, reports the FBI.

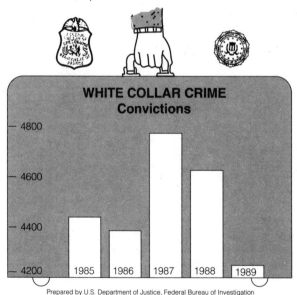

Prepared by U.S. Department of Justice, Federal Bureau of Investigation

The BBB Works with Business

During nearly 80 years of operation, the Council of Better Business Bureaus and its network of local BBBs have documented thousands of cases in which businesses have suffered at the hands of con artists and schemers. The victims include a wide variety of businesses, from neighborhood "mom-and-pop" stores to multinational conglomerates.

You Are Not Defenseless

The stereotypical armed bandit is becoming of almost secondary concern as, increasingly, culprits turn out to be trusted employees, family members, or friends. This phenomenon demands a whole new manner of vigilance.

A little knowledge is a very useful thing when it comes to recognizing and foiling a fraud, scheme, or theft. While there are no foolproof solutions to the serious crime problems discussed in this book, you can keep losses to a minimum by knowing and applying these four basic principles:

- Be aware of your crime losses.

- Apply risk management techniques to prevent crimes before they occur.

- Train employees at all levels in crime recognition and prevention.

- Report all illegal activities to the appropriate law enforcement authorities.

This book describes how various schemes work, how you can detect them, how you can protect your business against con artists and schemers, and what legal recourses to use if you are victimized. Although there are areas in which the nature of operation of the various types of schemes overlaps, we have divided the white-collar crimes commonly committed against business into three categories.

Section I deals with "Schemes Against Business," including office supply schemes, phony invoice schemes, charity schemes, loan broker fraud, bankruptcy fraud, business opportunity schemes, and telemarketing crimes.

Section II, "External Crime," covers product counterfeiting, crimes practiced on cashiers, shoplifting, credit card fraud, check fraud, coupon fraud, cargo theft, and industrial espionage.

Section III addresses some of the fastest-growing and most damaging types of business crimes – "Internal Crime." This section covers pilferage and embezzlement; bribery, kick-backs, and payoffs; insurance fraud; and computer crime.

A book could be written on each of the topics covered. But we feel that it is more important for every businessperson to acquire a basic understanding of the most prevalent forms of the crimes that threaten their businesses. That knowledge is the first important step in learning how to stop, or at least reduce the risk of, crime against business.

Figuratively Speaking

In an effort to indicate the extent of losses sustained by the business community due to crimes directed against it, we have contacted numerous government agencies, business organizations and associations, law enforcement officials, and private monitoring groups. Nearly all of these groups caution that it is virtually impossible to compile totally accurate statistics in this area, the main barrier being the frequent nonreportage of crimes against business. The National Institute of Justice points out that some businesspeople who become aware that they are victims of crimes such as internal theft and fraud resolve these problems internally, never making their losses public; others write them off as an inevitable cost of doing business. Embarrassment also may discourage the reporting of crimes to public agencies or business groups. And, of course, there are the crimes that are never detected, often because businesspeople have not been trained to recognize the telltale signs. For whatever reason, many crimes against business never become part of official estimates, making many statistics little more than educated guesses. The figures we cite constitute the "best guesses" of a host of individuals and organizations, but the reader should be aware that even among the experts, figures often vary widely.

The Role of the BBB

Our goal is to help you avoid becoming the victim of the kinds of crime covered in this book. A special section in each chapter details your legal recourses and the appropriate agencies to contact if you are victimized, and Appendix A provides addresses and phone numbers for the agencies cited.

We urge you also to contact your local Better Business Bureau. Appendix B provides addresses and phone numbers for the 191 local BBBs in the U.S. and Canada.

Local Bureaus assist businesses and consumers through:

☐ **Pertinent information.** Each local Bureau keeps files on large numbers of firms and organizations in its service area. BBBs provide basic information such as how long a firm has been in business, whether or not customers or other businesses have filed complaints, and the nature of the complaints and the manner in which the firm resolved them. BBBs can also provide factual information on local and national charitable organizations.

☐ **Complaint handling.** Acting as impartial third parties, BBBs use arbitration and mediation to find mutually acceptable solutions to disputes between businesses and consumers.

☐ **Checks on advertising claims.** BBBs regularly monitor advertisements and investigate misleading or inaccurate claims. In addition, the Bureaus handle complaints from businesses concerning competitors' advertising.

☐ **Standards development.** Working with industry and business groups, the BBB develops voluntary advertising codes and standards.

How You Can Help

We hope that readers will bring to our attention schemes against business that are not covered in this book, as well as unusual variations of the crimes outlined in these pages. Only by working with you can we continue to assist you and your business colleagues in combatting our common enemy, crime against business. Please direct your comments to:

> Publications Department
> Council of Better Business Bureaus, Inc.
> 4200 Wilson Boulevard - Suite 800
> Arlington, VA 22203

SECTION I

SCHEMES AGAINST BUSINESS

CHAPTER 1

Office Supply Schemes and "Paper Pirates"

THE CASE OF
The Careless Copier

A call comes into a small business office from a representative of its "regular supplier of office products" and is passed along to the employee who operates the photocopier. The caller – ostensibly in order to "update her files" – requests verification of the make and model number of the company's photocopier and then explains that her records indicate it is time for the company to reorder supplies. Since shipments normally take a few weeks, she recommends the order be placed now. Lulled by the caller's smooth, matter-of-fact manner, the employee approves the order.

Several weeks later, the supplies arrive, directed to the attention of the employee who approved the order and who now approves the shipment by signing a delivery form. The subsequent invoice is also okayed by the employee, who assures the accounting department that the supplies have been received. The bill is promptly paid and the supplies are placed in storage.

During a periodic maintenance call, a technician from the manufacturer of the machine notices the boxes of photocopier supplies and sternly informs the office manager that the use of these "off-brand" supplies could harm the equipment and invalidate the company's warranty. A look at the records reveals that the company has never before done business with this "off-brand" supplier, and when the office manager tries to return the supplies for a refund, the supply company responds that returns are against its policy. Besides, the delivery form, signed by a company employee, clearly states, "All sales final."

Unethical But Legal Sales Pitches

Every year, millions of dollars' worth of high-quality, fairly priced office supplies are sold over the telephone by honest, reputable suppliers. Unfortunately for many businesses and organizations, millions of dollars are also conned out of U.S. businesses each year by office supply schemers and "paper pirates" or "toner-phoners" like the one described above. The National Office Products Association estimates annual business losses at $50 million but notes that figures could actually be much higher. The large majority of these rip-offs go either undetected or unreported because the supplies are used or the victims are embarrassed to acknowledge they've been taken.

Even when the victim is aware of the swindle, in many cases there is no legal recourse. While their schemes might be highly unethical, the perpetrators usually devise them in a manner that is totally legal. Telephone salespeople for these unethical operations are carefully trained not to misrepresent their employers, and their meticulously scripted pitches avoid identifying their operations with brand name suppliers or manufacturers.

This is not to say that swindlers can't mislead the hapless target on the other end of the telephone by, for example, offering to sell photocopier toner "for your ABC copier"–not at all the same thing as "ABC toner." Some hustlers also package their off-brand supplies to look like brand name products.

"WATS-line Hustlers"

Paper pirate and office supply schemes frequently operate from ramshackle supply warehouses thousands of miles from their prospective victims. For their use of long-distance telephone lines, such as the Wide Area Telecommunications Service, or WATS-line, these solicitors have been dubbed "WATS-line hustlers" by law enforcement officials.

According to the Federal Trade Commission (FTC), typical WATS-line hustlers target all kinds of businesses and organizations, including restaurants, professional offices, religious groups, schools, and hospitals. They generally sell products needing constant replacement, such as office supplies (pens; typewriter ribbons; fax paper; photocopier paper, ink or toner) and maintenance supplies (light bulbs, cleaning compounds).

The telephone solicitors often read from printed scripts and use a printed list of responses to deflect objections.

While WATS-line hustlers use many different ploys, the FTC identifies the following common tactics:

☐ **They rarely deal with the authorized purchasing agent**. WATS-line hustlers usually try to talk with an employee who is unfamiliar with purchasing procedures, e.g., an inexperienced clerk, secretary, or maintenance person. They may use the name of the authorized purchasing agent or of another employee to convince the unwitting victim to divulge information or approve an order.

☐ **They may mislead you to solicit an order.** WATS-line hustlers usually try to mislead you into believing that they represent your regular supplier. The National Office Products Association cautions that one effective scam involves the fraudulent use of the name of a business's actual supplier to solicit orders. Hustlers also have been known to introduce themselves as representing a storage company with an impressive-sounding name such as U.S. General Storage or American Central Warehouse.

☐ **They might try to con you with a fabricated tale of a "disaster"** that allows them to offer substantial savings by selling supplies at sharply reduced prices. Overturned tractor-trailers, fire sales, and liquidations are among the many fictions used.

☐ **They may claim to be conducting a survey of office equipment or updating their records.** Once you have given them the information they need (for example, the model number on your photocopier), they may pose as your new supplier or as an authorized dealer for the products you use.

☐ **They may try to pressure you into placing an immediate order.** WATS-line hustlers may offer "bargain prices" if you order right away – but their prices are usually no bargain. The pitch that prices are "going up tomorrow" or that, since you mistakenly were not notified of a price increase, you are entitled to a special "one-time-only" purchase at the "old" price, is aimed at pushing you into immediate, imprudent action.

☐ **They may offer free gifts.** To induce you to place an order, WATS-line hustlers may offer to send a free personal gift, such as a transistor radio or calculator, to your home. Most likely, the gift will never arrive, and even if it does, its value will rarely be offset by the inflated price of the products ordered.

☐ **They may misrepresent merchandise,** including the quality, type, size, and brand of their products.

☐ **They may refuse to accept returned merchandise.** If you complain about the products received, WATS-line hustlers may try to persuade you to keep the shipment at a so-called "discount price." They usually refuse to accept returned merchandise or pay for return shipments, and they may attempt to charge you for storage or damages.

HOW TO PROTECT YOUR BUSINESS

Because there are so many variations of the paper pirate and office supply swindles, it is impossible to anticipate and guard against every possible approach. But there are steps you can take to keep your company from being victimized.

1. Never buy from a new supplier by telephone or mail until you have verified its existence and reliability. Ask for references and check them, find out how long the firm has operated out of its present location (and, if possible, visit the company), and ask your local BBB (see Appendix B) for a report.

2. Do not accept Cash on Delivery (COD) shipments. Insist on open account billing; that way, if there's a problem, you have some leverage.

3. Insist on sending written purchase orders.

4. Designate purchasing agents for ordering, receiving, and paying for supplies.

5. Inform all employees about your organization's purchasing, receiving, invoicing, and payment systems. Alert employees to the office supply racket and advise them not to give out information on makes and models of office equipment over the phone. Also, watch out for cold calls asking for verification of the name of the office manager or any other employee likely to make supply purchases.

WHAT TO DO IF YOU ARE VICTIMIZED

If you think you have been the victim of a paper pirate or office supply scheme, the Better Business Bureau recommends that you first contact the supplier and attempt to work out an amicable solution. If the supplier is uncooperative, your next step will depend on the stage at which you become aware of the scheme.

Unpaid-for Merchandise

If you have not paid for the merchandise and you feel that it has been misrepresented, withhold payment and do not use the merchandise.

Then take the following steps:

1. Send a certified letter to the company explaining your position and how you expect the company to settle the matter, e.g., by taking back the merchandise.

2. If the firm fails to respond within your stated period of time, send a copy of your letter to your local Better Business Bureau (see Appendix B), with a cover letter asking the BBB for assistance.

3. If the problem remains unresolved, notify your local police department and the nearest office of the FTC (see Appendix A). If the U.S. mail has been used in any way by the organization attempting to defraud you, contact the Chief Postal Inspector, U.S. Postal Service (see Appendix A).

4. If at this stage the supplier threatens to take legal action or to turn your account over to a collection agency, contact an attorney and your state attorney general's office, listed under state government in most telephone directories.

5. You may also want to contact the National Office Machine Dealers Association (see Appendix A), which can provide counsel in returning unordered office supplies and filing complaints with the FTC and state attorney general.

Unordered Merchandise Sent by U.S. Mail

1. Under federal law, you are entitled to regard unordered merchandise sent through the U.S. mail as a free gift. The same law makes it illegal to mail bills for such unordered merchandise. Note, however, that this does not include merchandise sent in error.

2. You are entitled to refuse a shipment arriving by U.S. mail as long as you don't open it. To avoid misunderstandings, first send the company shipping the merchandise a letter (preferably certified with return receipt requested) asking for proof of your order.

3. If you are positive the merchandise was not ordered, write the shipper that you are keeping it as a free gift and sending a copy of your letter to the FTC. Keep copies of all correspondence for your records.

Unordered Merchandise Sent by Private Delivery Services

1. If unordered merchandise arrives by private delivery, do not accept the shipment.

2. If you have already accepted the shipment, send the shipper a certified letter with return receipt requested, demanding proof of your order. If there is no valid proof, inform the sender that unless the merchandise is picked up within thirty days, you will dispose of it. By giving the sender an opportunity to recover the merchandise, you invalidate any claim that you accepted an offer of sale merely by keeping the shipment.

3. If you return the merchandise, do so at the sender's expense and get a receipt from the carrier.

4. If an invoice for the unordered merchandise arrives, withhold payment and do not use the merchandise. If the firm fails to respond to your letter, contact your local Better Business Bureau for assistance.

5. If the BBB cannot help you resolve the problem, notify your local police department and the nearest office of the FTC.

6. If the supplier threatens you with legal action, contact an attorney and your state attorney general's office.

When They Insist You Placed an Order

1. WATS-line hustlers often insist that an order was placed and verified. Before you accept or pay for any merchandise that arrives under less-than-clear circumstances, protect yourself by insisting on proof that an order was placed. If no proof is forthcoming, follow the appropriate steps listed above.

2. If you believe the sender made an honest mistake, you may offer to return the goods at the sender's expense.

3. If it turns out that a verifiable order was placed and you have received exactly what was ordered, you are responsible for paying the bill.

CHAPTER 2

Phony Invoice Schemes

 THE CASE OF
The Bogus Bill

The head of maintenance for a large chain of department stores receives a call from the "governor's energy office." As part of an "official survey" of the state's most energy efficient businesses, the caller would like to ask some questions about the department store chain's efforts to reduce energy consumption.

The maintenance chief is flattered to receive a call from a high-level official. Proudly, he describes his company's conscientious efforts, including a new program of phasing in energy efficient light bulbs. The caller's respectful inquiries elicit all the details: when bulbs are replaced, how many, what type, at what cost.

Several weeks later, shortly after the chain has completed its most recent bulb replacement, the accounting department receives an invoice for light bulbs. The bill contains all the correct details of the company's normal quarterly supply, including the name of the head of maintenance as originator of the order.

With everything appearing to be in order, the bill is processed through accounting and paid. It isn't until two weeks later, when a second bill for exactly the same purchase arrives, that some serious questions are raised. Accounting discovers, much to its chagrin, that while this new bill is legitimate, the first was not. To make matters worse, the check sent in payment of the first invoice has been cashed. And the firm is no longer at the listed address.

Anatomy of a Scam

Phony invoicing schemes, of which the above story is one example, typically prey on the inefficiency of targeted businesses. For their successful execution, these schemes rely on sloppy bookkeeping, inattention on the part of employees, and perhaps most importantly, the failure of one arm of a business to know what the other arm is doing.

The U.S. Postal Service believes that con artists succeed in collecting a significant percentage of all the bills they mail but notes that due to the nature of the crime, it is impossible to determine the exact extent of losses. While law enforcement officials are unable to place an actual dollar figure on the amount swindled each year, the fact that this type of swindler mails thousands of phony invoices and solicitations disguised as invoices on a regular basis points to an annual loss to businesses that may run into billions of dollars.

While there is no set formula for these invoice schemes, most involve the use of an initial telephone contact. The call helps the swindler obtain the names of key business contacts as well as some important details about the operation of the business and its products or services.

The persons making these calls are, for the most part, remarkably smooth operators. Often brazen and forward in their approach, they have been known to talk their way through a chain of receptionists, secretaries, assistant managers, supervisors, and vice presidents to gain access to heads of companies. In most cases, however, they need gain access to only lower-level employees.

The con artist's next contact with the intended victim commonly comes in the form of a phony invoice sent through the mail. The invoice, which includes names, figures, and other details that add to the appearance of legitimacy, may be paid unwittingly along with a number of other routine bills. In many cases, the amount of the invoice is just small enough to slip by the check writer's attention. The swindler has had considerable experience calculating the most effective dollar amount, depending on variables such as the size of the firm and the control it seems to have on its management system. Thousands of mass-mailed invoices, each for a small sum may prove more lucrative than several large invoices.

Scare tactics sometimes are used to increase the odds of success. A phony invoice or past-due notice stamped "Pay This Bill Now" or "We Are About to Start Action" may intimidate the victim into rushing to make out a check without carefully investigating the supposedly delinquent charge.

Individual consumers also may be victimized by phony invoice schemes through fraudulent invoices mailed to their homes. One common twist on the scheme is mailing solicitations and phony invoices disguised as government documents. These mailings use seals, insignias, and copycat names similar to the names of federal agencies to induce recipients to purchase or pay for a product or service or to contribute funds or membership fees. And to compound the injury, beleaguered victims of phony invoice schemes, whether individuals or businesses, are quickly identified once they pay and are often flooded with additional invoices for nonexistent subscriptions, supplies, and services.

Solicitations in the Guise of Invoices

One of the most common variations of the phony invoice scheme is issuing solicitations disguised as invoices. These documents, which are actually solicitations for the purchase of goods or services, are carefully designed to look like legitimate invoices for goods or services ordered and received. In some cases, the small print may identify the bogus bill as a solicitation. The business that pays a solicitation disguised as an invoice may receive the merchandise or service it was duped into ordering; more often, it will not, and efforts to trace the fraudulent firm that issued the "invoice" will prove futile.

The deceptive solicitation may be received through the mail or may be presented in person by a con artist who visits a business office on the pretext of saving the company handling charges. In the case of *phony advertising solicitations,* the "advertising salesperson" may make the transaction seem routine, asking if the business wishes to renew an ad allegedly placed "last year." Often the invoice is supported by fabricated proof of the ad's placement – a trumped-up "clipping" created by the con artist using an actual company ad.

Most advertising solicitation schemes involve the issuing of invoices for ads in magazines, newspapers, or directories targeted at specific ethnic or special-interest groups. The promoter may try to manipulate the victim's emotions or create embarrassment in order to sell an ad in an ethnic-oriented publication. Often the pitch includes the implication that part of the advertising revenues will be used to support community programs. In another twist, the businessperson, fearful of appearing uncooperative, may be pressured into placing an ad in a phony law enforcement publication.

One telltale sign of the advertising solicitation scheme is the unusually flexible salesperson who quickly reduces the advertising rates when a customer seems hesitant.

We Are Now About To Start Action

DIRECTED TO THE ATTENTION OF

MARK MORRIS

AUTHORIZED

RKM

THEME ISSUE

VETERANS

SPECIAL COPY CONTENTS

YEARBOOK, VETERANS SALUTE   AMOUNT DUE $89.20

MAILING ADDRESS 35 Sandrock Ave., New York,

USE ENCLOSED ENVELOPE FOR YOUR CHECK TO PAY THIS BILL NOW

PAY THIS BILL NOW

FILE COPY

Bogus Yellow Pages Bills

Let your eyes do the walking, not your fingers, if you receive an invoice for renewing your advertisement in a local business directory. U.S. Postal Inspectors and Better Business Bureaus across the country are looking into a new and alarmingly widespread scam in which solicitations disguised as invoices for yellow pages listings are being mailed to businesses by hundreds of copycat directory publishers. These misleading solicitations, usually for about $100, fall just short of actually breaking the law. Most include the disclaimers required by federal postal law to distinguish a solicitation from an invoice. But many recipients don't read the fine print, and many are misled by the names of the soliciting companies, which resemble those of the well-known business directory distributors, and by the familiar walking fingers logo. Use of the logo is not illegal, since neither the logo nor the term yellow pages is a registered trademark.

Most of the soliciting firms publish a directory of sorts, but the value and circulation of these publications are questionable at best. The targets of the solicitations usually are selected from ads placed in local yellow pages directories, and some solicitations even include clippings of bona fide yellow pages ads. The misleading solicitations may be stamped "Renewal" or "Amount Due" and may warn that businesses failing to pay promptly will be left out of the next telephone directory.

The BBB advises businesses receiving "invoices" for yellow pages listings to scrutinize them carefully. If in doubt, contact your local BBB for a report on the soliciting company. And remember that, with few exceptions, charges for legitimate directory listings are included in advertisers' monthly phone bills, not billed separately.

Fax directory schemes. Your company receives an official-looking invoice requesting payment for a listing in an international business telefax or telex directory. Be on the alert: The "invoice" may be a solicitation in disguise, issued by one of the many fraudulent "directory companies" across the U.S. and overseas. Often, the directory does not even exist. In fact, the fine print on the invoice may simply indicate an intention to print the directory – making legal recourse nearly impossible if you find out about the scam only after you've paid the bill. To further complicate matters, the address to which you are directed to mail your check, often a post office box, may be nothing more than a mail drop.

To avoid getting taken by a phony fax directory firm, make certain your accounting department is aware of the scheme. Follow the steps outlined in this chapter to protect your business and to report any suspicious invoices received. And remember, legitimate fax directory publishers generally do not charge for listings; some, in fact, ensure a steady flow of new listings by offering cash or prizes for new fax numbers.

HOW TO PROTECT YOUR BUSINESS

The best protection against invoice frauds or schemes is knowledge and vigilance. Your company's accounting department or the individuals responsible for paying bills should be made aware of solicitations disguised as invoices and for other dubious bills from unfamiliar companies.

Specifically, observe the following precautions:

1. Never place an order over the telephone unless there is no doubt that the firm you are dealing with is reputable. Get the organization's name, address, and phone number, as well as its representative's full name and position. If a significant amount of money is involved, ask for business and local bank references and check them. Find out how long the firm has operated out of its present location. If possible, visit the company or firm. Ask your local Better Business Bureau (see Appendix B) for a report.

2. Check your records to confirm claims of previous business dealings.

3. Before placing advertising, verify that the publication exists and that its circulation suits your needs. Circulation figures can be verified by contacting the Audit Bureau of Circulations (see Appendix A).

4. Establish effective internal controls for the payment of invoices.

   - Channel all bills through one department.

   - Insist that employees fill out prenumbered purchase orders for every order placed.

   - Check all invoices against purchase orders and against goods or services received. Make certain that order numbers correspond.

   - Verify all invoices with the person who gave written or verbal authorization.

   - Clear all invoices with the appropriate executives.

   - If the invoicing company claims to have a tape recording of the order, insist on hearing it.

Know the Law

Federal law is clear-cut and specific in its position on solicitations. It is against U.S. Postal Service regulations to mail a bill, invoice, or statement of account due that is actually a solicitation, unless it bears one of the following disclaimers:

> THIS IS A SOLICITATION FOR THE ORDER OF GOODS OR SERVICES, OR BOTH, AND NOT A BILL, INVOICE, OR STATEMENT OF ACCOUNT DUE. YOU ARE UNDER NO OBLIGATION TO MAKE ANY PAYMENTS ON ACCOUNT OF THIS OFFER UNLESS YOU ACCEPT THIS OFFER.

or

> THIS IS NOT A BILL. THIS IS A SOLICITATION. YOU ARE UNDER NO OBLIGATION TO PAY UNLESS YOU ACCEPT THIS OFFER.

One of these disclaimers must be conspicuously printed on the face of the solicitation in at least 30-point type. That is type

THIS BIG

Print colors must be reproducible on copying machines and cannot be obscured by folding or other means. If the solicitation is more than one page, the disclaimer must appear on each page, and if it is perforated, the required language must appear on each section that could be construed as a bill. Regulations prohibit any language that modifies or qualifies the disclaimer, such as "legal notice required by law."

Regulations regarding copycat "government documents" – solicitations by nongovernmental entities that use a seal, insignia, trade or brand name, or any other term or symbol that implies a federal government connection or endorsement, require the following disclaimer to appear, in conspicuous and legible type, on the face of the solicitation:

> THIS ORGANIZATION [or PRODUCT or SERVICE] HAS NOT BEEN APPROVED OR ENDORSED BY THE FEDERAL GOVERNMENT, AND THIS OFFER IS NOT BEING MADE BY AN AGENCY OF THE FEDERAL GOVERNMENT

In addition, the mailing envelope or outside wrapper must bear this disclaimer, in capital letters and in conspicuous and legible type:

> THIS IS NOT A GOVERNMENT DOCUMENT

Mailing solicitations that do not meet these requirements can result in a U.S. Postal Service stop order under which responses are returned to the sender, cutting off the soliciting firm's source of revenue.

Other forms of phony invoice schemes may involve mail fraud or may violate other federal postal regulations.

WHAT TO DO IF YOU ARE VICTIMIZED

If you receive a phony invoice or a solicitation disguised as an invoice, use the following procedure to report the matter to the U.S. Postal Service and your local Better Business Bureau:

1. On the envelope in which the phony invoice or solicitation arrived, note the date received and sign your name. Be sure all the solicitation material is returned to the envelope in which it was received.

2. Prepare a notarized affidavit. See the following sample, page 36.

3. Send the solicitation material and the original affidavit to the Chief Postal Inspector, U.S. Postal Service (see Appendix A). Keep a copy for your records, and send a copy to your local Better Business Bureau (see Appendix B).

If you become aware of the scheme only after payments have been made on the fraudulent invoices, immediately contact the Chief Postal Inspector, your local police department, and the BBB. In most cases, you will be instructed to stop payment on your check or money order. The postal authorities should also inform you if any recourse is possible. If potential losses are considerable, contact your attorney for help in expediting your case.

TO: Chief Postal Inspector
      Attn: Fraud Section
      United States Postal Service
      Washington, D.C. 20260

AFFIDAVIT

I, _____

being duly sworn, depose and say:

1. I am _____ of _____
              (position)   (company)

   located at _____ .
                          (address and zip code)

2. On or about _____ our firm received
                          (date)

   through the United States mail a solicitation from

   _____

   _____
                        (name and address)

   which resembles a bill, invoice, or statement of account.

3. I have dated and signed the solicitation material and
   enclosed it herewith.

4. Our firm has never done business with _____

   _____
                            (name)

   and we have not requested a listing or authorized the
   insertion of our advertisement in the publication
   referred to in the solicitation.

5. It is my opinion that the subject solicitation represents
   an attempt to elicit a remittance from my firm by means
   of deception.   _____
                                            (signature)

Subscribed and sworn to before me this _____ day of

_____ , _____

_____

My commission expires _____

CHAPTER 3

Charitable Solicitation Schemes

THE CASE OF
The Uninformed Donor

A well-dressed man introducing himself as a representative of a nonprofit organization that helps families in need visits a corporate office. Meeting with a company executive, the man discusses the specific needs of the families his organization assists. He hands the executive a glossy brochure with pictures of the families and graphic descriptions of their privations. Also included in the brochure is a chart showing the amounts of money considered "fair" contributions from companies of varying sizes.

After conferring with "higher-ups," the executive agrees to donate a company check for the requested amount. The executive and other company officials are satisfied that their business has done its part to help the needy families in its community. What they don't know is that less than 10 percent of their contribution will actually help families in need. The remainder will go toward paying high salaries for the fund raisers and extravagant overhead charges for the organization.

Corporate Contributions to Charity

American businesses regularly are asked for donations to worthy causes. According to the American Association of Fund Raising Counsel, $5.9 billion in money and merchandise was contributed to charitable causes by American corporations in 1990, an increase of 5.4 percent over 1989. It is impossible to say how much of this goes to support the cause as the contributor intended.

While a cautious examination of charitable appeals clearly is in order, many people find it difficult to refuse a request for help. Some businesspeople are sensitive to the needs of the community; others are afraid of appearing cold-blooded by turning down a request; some even fear neighborhood resistance or boycotts from their customers – the very people upon whom they depend for their livelihood.

Despite such concerns, careful evaluation of charitable solicitations – and rejection of those pleas that fail to meet standards – is not only a smart business practice but is one of the responsibilities of the community-minded business. Deceptive charity pleas defraud businesses and consumers and injure legitimate, more cost-effective and responsible charitable groups by undermining their efforts to raise funds for truly worthwhile causes.

 HOW TO PROTECT YOUR BUSINESS

The most effective way a business or individual can have a positive impact on society through charitable giving is by becoming a well-informed giver. When you consider contributions of your or your employer's money, merchandise, name, or time, make sure the donation will serve the purpose you intend.

Organizations that approach businesses or the public for charitable contributions should provide, upon request, all the information that a potential donor might reasonably wish to consider. In close and extensive contacts with legitimate charitable organizations, the Better Business Bureau has found that responsible groups are willing to provide such information.

You usually can obtain reliable information by requesting and reviewing a copy of the charity's complete annual report and financial statements.

These reports should provide:

1. The full name and permanent address of the organization.

2. A clear description of the organization's purposes.

3. Descriptions of programs and activities.

4. A list of accomplishments.

5. Information about the governing body and its structure.

6. Details of management and staff responsibilities and services.

7. An elaboration on its legal eligibility to receive tax deductible contributions. (Keep in mind that *tax exempt* is not the same as *tax deductible*. See pages 40 to 42.)

8. Information about financial activities, such as income, fund-raising costs, and financial position.

Examine the financial information provided by the organization to be certain that the statements have been audited in accordance with generally accepted accounting principles. Other specifics to look for include a breakdown of expenses into categories of programs, fund-raising, and management; a detailed schedule of expenses, such as salaries, employee benefits, travel expenses, and mailing; and notes about business transactions with board members. In particular, determine approximately what percentage of public contributions are applied to the programs and activities described in the solicitation.

The Philanthropic Service of the Council of Better Business Bureaus recommends that at least 50 percent of a charity's total income from all sources be spent on programs and activities directly related to the organization's purposes. In addition, fund-raising costs should not exceed 35 percent of related contributions. In applying these guidelines, however, donors should consider extenuating circumstances, such as unusual bequests, donor restrictions on the use of funds, and the unique expenses of a newly founded organization.

IRS Rules on Tax Deductible Donations

If an organization declares it is "tax exempt," it means that the organization does not have to pay taxes. However, not all contributions to tax exempt organizations are deductible for federal income tax purposes.

The Internal Revenue Service defines more than twenty different categories of tax exempt organizations. Contributions to only a few of these are also tax deductible.

Organizations that are tax exempt under section 501(c)(3) of the Internal Revenue Code are broadly termed **"charitable"** organizations. Organizations in this category include the following types of nonprofit groups: charitable, religious, educational, scientific, literary, those that work to prevent cruelty to children and animals, and those that foster national or international amateur sports competition. Contributions to these organizations are deductible as charitable donations for federal income tax purposes.

Other tax exempt groups include **civic leagues** and **social welfare** organizations that are tax exempt under section 501(c)(4) of the Internal Revenue Code and **business membership** organizations that are exempt under 501(c)(6). Contributions to such organizations are not deductible as charitable donations for federal income tax purposes but might be deductible as a business expense.

A special category for **veterans'** organizations is the 501(c)(19) section. (Some older war veterans' organizations are tax exempt under section 501(c)(4), the previous designation for veterans' organizations.) Contributions to veterans' organizations are deductible as charitable donations

Police and firefighter organizations can be tax exempt under a number of different sections of the Internal Revenue Code, depending on the organization's purpose and structure. For example, contributions to volunteer fire departments that are tax exempt under section 501(c)(3) or 501(c)(4) of the Internal Revenue Code are deductible as charitable donations. However, contributions to police fraternal organizations that are tax exempt under sections 501(c)(8) or 501(c)(10) are only deductible as charitable donations if the contribution is to be used exclusively for charitable purposes.

If you are unsure about an organization's tax exempt status, ask the organization for a copy of its IRS "determination letter." Every group receives such a letter from the IRS when exempt status is granted. If you would like more information about tax exemption and deductions, contact your local IRS office.

What Can You Deduct?

Fair market value. If you donate property to a qualified organization, you generally may deduct only the fair market value of the property at the time of contribution. Fair market value is the price at which property would change hands between willing and reasonably knowledgeable buyers and sellers. IRS Publication 561, *Determining The Value of Donated Property** gives complete instructions for determining fair market value.

Benefits received. If you contribute to a charitable organization and also receive a benefit from it, you can deduct only the amount that is more than the value of the benefit you receive. For example, dues paid to a qualified organization may merely cover the cost of benefits you receive and are thus not deductible. If, however, the dues are actually a contribution for which you receive little or no benefit in return, the amount in excess of any benefits received is deductible. Similarly, if you buy tickets from a qualified organization for a charity ball, banquet, sporting event, etc., you can deduct only the amount that is more than the established charge for the event. Whether you use the tickets or other privileges has no effect on the amount you may deduct.

The cost of the benefit and/or the amount in excess of costs should be disclosed by the charitable organization. Keep in mind, though, that a ticket or other proof of payment may indicate that your payment is a "contribution" without necessarily meaning that you can deduct the full amount. For example, the ticket for a benefit show may be stamped "Contribution – $40." If the regular price for the show is $8, however, your deductible contribution is only $32.

If you receive only token items, such as a bookmark or a cap, in connection with your payment, you may be able to deduct the entire payment as a charitable contribution. In this case, the charity must notify you that the item you receive is of insubstantial value and that the payment can be deducted in full.

*You can order IRS publications and forms by calling 800-TAX FORM.

Out-of-pocket expenses. You cannot deduct the value of your volunteer time or services to a charity. However, some out-of-pocket expenses paid in giving service can be deducted. These include most unreimbursed travel and transportation expenses.

When can you deduct? Contributions are deductible for the year in which they are actually paid or unconditionally delivered, as by mail. Pledges are not deductible until the year paid.

Shows That Benefit Charities

Charities will sometimes hire professional fund raisers that produce traveling circuses or variety shows as special fund-raising events. Typically, after an agreement is reached, a fund-raising firm sells tickets for the show. In many instances, a solicitor will state that if you aren't interested in attending the show, you can purchase tickets that will be distributed to handicapped or underprivileged children in your area. If such statements are made, don't hesitate to ask the solicitor how many such children there are, how they were chosen, how many tickets for the children have been sold, how the tickets will be distributed to such children, and if transportation to the event will be provided. In many communities, the number of children "eligible" to receive free tickets is limited and transportation to the event is not arranged. So, in effect, free tickets given to a few needy children who attend the event might have been paid for many times over by the businesses and individuals who have bought the tickets.

In addition, depending on the details of the written agreement between the charity and the promoter, the nonprofit organization might receive only a small portion (in some cases less than 20 percent) of the total money raised through ticket sales. The charity or the promoter should identify at the point of solicitation the actual or anticipated portion of the ticket price that will benefit the cause. If the solicitor doesn't offer this information outright, ask for it.

Canisters on the Counter

Businesses that are open to the public are often asked to place coin canisters or display cards in an accessible area so that customers can donate their change to a charitable cause. If your business is asked to participate in such a fund-raising effort, don't hesitate to ask the nonprofit organization for more information about its location and the nature of its programs. Look at the container and make sure it includes a clear description of the programs for which funds are being raised and an address that donors or potential donors can use to request more information. Find out if the organization will regularly send a representative to collect filled canisters or if your business will be responsible for either contacting the charity or mailing the collected funds. Also remember that closed containers help ensure greater control over the loss or theft of these types of contributions.

Advertising in Charity Publications

Your business might be solicited to place an ad in a charity's newspaper, journal, or magazine. If so, verify the type of organization selling the ad. Even though it might have a name that sounds like that of a charitable organization, the publication in fact could be published by a for-profit company.

Do not hesitate to ask for the same information you would want to consider before any ad placement. How many copies of the publication will be printed? Who will receive it? Does the publication cost anything? How often is it printed? What is the estimated publication date? Will this publication be distributed to the number and the kinds of people your business wants to reach?

You might also want to ask the organization if it hired a promoter to produce the publication and/or sell ad space. If so, only a portion of the proceeds from the ad sales will benefit the charity. If you decide to place an ad, ask for a copy of both the draft and final published version of the ad.

You might receive an invoice for an ad without having placed an order. If this happens, remember there are laws and regulations against this type of deception. (See page 29, "Solicitations in the Guise of Invoices.")

Remember that the cost of placing a business ad in a charity's publication is not deductible as a charitable donation but may be deductible as a business expense if it can be shown that the expense is "ordinary" and "necessary" in carrying out your trade or business. If the ad is in the form of a personal message or greeting, it might not be deductible.

Charity-Business Marketing

Tens of millions of dollars will be raised for charities during the 1990s as a result of the explosive growth in charity-business marketing arrangements. Charities participating in such promotional partnerships with for-profit corporations now are featured in everything from television commercials to Sunday newspaper supplement coupons. The basic message, "BUY THE PRODUCT OF CORPORATION ABC AND A CONTRIBUTION WILL BE MADE TO CHARITY XYZ," has become so pervasive that U.S. consumers are confronted with a number of charity-business marketing appeals each day.

Voluntary CBBB standards call for charities to establish and exercise controls over fund-raising activities conducted for their benefit and to include certain information in solicitations made in conjunction with the sale of goods or services. Participants in joint-venture marketing who wish to ensure the charitable organization's compliance with these standards should follow these recommendations:

1. A written agreement between the company and the charity should give the corporation formal permission to use the charity's name and logo, and the charity prior review and approval of all joint-venture solicitations that use the charity's name.

2. Joint-venture advertisements should specify:

   - The portion of the product or service price or the fixed amount per sale/transaction to benefit the charity and, if applicable, the maximum amount the charity will receive.

   - The full name of the charity.

   - An address or phone number to contact for additional information about the charity or the campaign.

   - The term of the campaign.

Your Good Name

Contributing money is only one of the ways in which you and your business may be asked to assist charitable groups. Other common approaches include requests that you serve as sponsor or nominal head of a fund-raising drive, give your time as a volunteer or neighborhood solicitor, or serve on the board of a charitable organization.

When you allow your name or your company's name to be used by an organization, it is assumed that you also are lending your active support to its activities and fund-raising procedures. Your reputation is on the line.Therefore, it is doubly important that you secure detailed information on the program, its resources, and its fund-raising methods before agreeing to provide such support.

Even if you are only a minor contributor, you may want to think twice before allowing a charitable group to use your company's name. Some organizations have been known to use the names of contributors to pressure others to contribute.

If you decide to agree to the use of your company's name, ask for a signed agreement clearly specifying how, when, and where it may be used and confirming your right to review and approve advance copies of all print and audio visual materials that contain references to your company. Soliciting organizations should honor requests for confidentiality and should not publicize the identity of donors without prior written permission. Organizations that violate this trust should be brought to the attention of local Better Business Bureaus and the Council of Better Business Bureaus' Philanthropic Advisory Service (see Appendix B).

Offers of Merchandise

When asked to buy merchandise, services, or tickets to a fund-raising event in support of a worthy cause, consider whether you would make the purchase if there were no charitable pitch. If not, consider whether backing the event will provide the maximum benefit to those you want to help.

Be wary of approaches that ask you to commit your company to buying "four tickets again this year." Was there a "last year"? What is the nature of the event? Whom will the purchase help?

If you are not really interested in the offered item, service, or event but would like to help the organization, consider a direct contribution, the full amount of which would benefit the charity. Then send your check directly to the charity, not to the promotion office.

If you decide to make the purchase, remember that only part of the purchase price is tax deductible. Only the amount of money that exceeds what the Internal Revenue Service calls the "fair market value" of the item or service is considered a donation for tax purposes. For example, if you pay ten dollars for a box of candy that normally sells for eight dollars, only the two-dollar difference can be claimed as a charitable contribution. (See page 41, "Benefits Received.")

Some Final Tips

In considering charitable contributions, keep the following guidelines in mind:

- If your business is inundated with an ever-increasing number of appeals, consider developing a more carefully defined giving program. For example, you might decide how much you want to contribute during the year, identify a short list of "must" contributions, and then select one or two focal points for the firm's giving. Your company's focus should reflect its size, location, structure, the nature of its business objectives, and the needs of the community. You might also want to involve employees in the contributions decision process or give to programs in which employees themselves are involved.

- Ask questions, and do not contribute until you are satisfied with the answers. Charities with nothing to hide will encourage your interest. Be wary of those reluctant to answer reasonable questions.

- Don't succumb to pressure to give money on the spot. The charity that needs your money today will welcome it just as much tomorrow.

- Mail appeals should clearly identify the charity and describe its programs. Beware of appeals that bring tears to your eyes but tell you nothing about the charity or how its work addresses the problems depicted. Appeals should not be disguised as invoices. It is illegal to mail a bill or statement of account due that is in fact an appeal for funds, unless it bears a clear and noticeable disclaimer. See page 35 for guidelines on how to handle solicitations disguised as invoices.

- Mail appeals that include sweepstakes promotions should disclose that you do not have to contribute to be eligible for the prizes offered. Requiring a contribution would make the sweepstakes a lottery, and it is illegal to operate a lottery by mail.

- It is against the law to demand payment for unordered merchandise. If unordered items such as key rings, stamps, greeting cards, or pens are enclosed with an appeal letter, you are under no obligation to pay for or return the merchandise. See pages 24 and 25 for guidelines on handling cases involving unordered merchandise.

- Before buying candy, magazine subscriptions, cards, or tickets to a dinner or show to benefit a charity, ask what the charity's share will be. Keep in mind that only a portion of the amount paid for any such item may be deductible. And be wary of statements such as "all proceeds go to charity." That can mean that only the money left after expenses – which may be considerable – will go to the charitable cause.

- Don't be misled by a name that looks impressive or resembles the name of a well-known organization.

- Bear in mind that, although most states and many communities require charitable organizations to be registered with or licensed by state and local authorities, licensing does not mean that the government *endorses* the charity.

- Always make your contribution by check, and make the check out to the charity, not to the individual collecting the donation.

- Assign one staff person to handle all requests for charitable donations. This will save time and eliminate the possibility of duplicate donations.

- Keep records of your donations, such as receipts and cancelled checks, so you can document your charitable giving at tax time. Receipts and other written records should show the name of the organization and the date and amount of contribution. Although the value of your time as a volunteer is not deductible, out-of-pocket expenses that directly relate to your volunteer services, such as transportation costs, may be deductible.

- Check out local soliciting organizations with your local Better Business Bureau and with the local charity registration office (usually a division of the state attorney general's office). For information on national fund-raising organizations, contact the Philanthropic Advisory Service of the Council of Better Business Bureaus.

- Call your local Better Business Bureau and local police department if a fund raiser uses high-pressure tactics, such as intimidation, threats of public exposure or economic retaliation, or repeated and harassing phone calls or visits.

WHAT TO DO IF YOU ARE VICTIMIZED

If you believe you have been the victim of a deceptive charity plea, you can file a complaint against the soliciting organization by contacting your local Better Business Bureau (see Appendix B), the Internal Revenue Service (see Appendix A), or your state attorney general's office, listed under state government in most telephone directories. Complaints about national charities may be directed to the Council of Better Business Bureaus' Philanthropic Advisory Service. If the deception involved use of the U.S. mail, you also can file a complaint with the U.S. Postal Service (see Appendix A).

Many states have consumer protection agencies and special offices to regulate charities. See your telephone directory listings under state government.

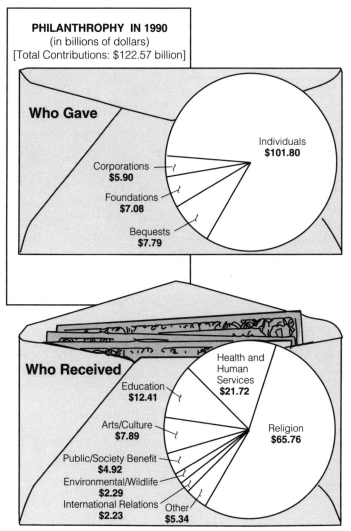

PHILANTHROPHY IN 1990
(in billions of dollars)
[Total Contributions: $122.57 billion]

Who Gave

Individuals
$101.80

Corporations
$5.90

Foundations
$7.08

Bequests
$7.79

Who Received

Health and
Human
Services
$21.72

Religion
$65.76

Education
$12.41

Arts/Culture
$7.89

Public/Society Benefit
$4.92

Environmental/Wildlife
$2.29

International Relations
$2.23

Other
$5.34

Source: American Association of Fund Raising Counsel, Inc.

CHAPTER 4

Loan Broker Frauds and "Advance Fee" Schemes

 THE CASE OF
The Vanishing Broker

A midwestern farmer needs funds to upgrade his business by installing a new, highly mechanized irrigation system. Unfortunately, due to cash flow problems and unexpected personal expenses, he is in arrears with his mortgage and tractor loan payments. Scanning the business section of his Sunday newspaper, he spots a small ad offering loans on a "non-secured basis to creditworthy individuals." He calls the listed phone number and makes an appointment.

At a suite in an airport hotel, the farmer meets a "loan broker" who listens to the details of his farm improvement plan and assures him that his enterprise is precisely the type for which a loan can be secured. The broker fills out several official-looking "loan application'" forms, which the farmer signs. A check for $15,000 will be on its way, the broker assures the farmer, within ten working days. All that is needed is the "agreed-upon" check for $875 in "advance loan fees" plus another $125 to process the loan.

Although the farmer is startled to hear that he must pay $1,000 to get the loan, the broker assures him this is standard practice. They agree to meet the following day – time enough for the farmer to float a temporary loan from relatives. The broker arranges to pick up a cashier's check for $1,000 at the farm. Two weeks pass, and the farmer, anxious because he hasn't heard from the broker, pulls out his copy of the loan agreement and calls the listed phone number. The phone has been disconnected. Further inquiry reveals that the post office box listed as the broker's local address has been closed.

How Legitimate Loan Brokers Work

Loan brokering is a legitimate business activity. But a growing number of businesspeople who have become discouraged by high interest rates and hard-to-find risk or investment capital are falling victim to swindlers operating loan broker schemes. The FBI estimates that each year American businesses are swindled out of millions of dollars by fraudulent loan brokers.

To examine how unscrupulous loan brokers practice their illegal schemes, we first must take a look at the way their legitimate counterparts operate.

Legitimate loan brokers generally are respected members of the business community who specialize in bringing together those in need of capital with those who have money to lend. The interest rate on these loans usually is several points higher than the prime interest rate, the rate that banks charge their top-rated corporate borrowers, with the actual figure determined by the loan's size and security.

A loan broker may or may not require what is called an "advance fee," or deposit, before providing any services. Even among legitimate brokers, advance fees are not uncommon, and they may not always be refundable, regardless of whether the loan is obtained. Some brokers promise a refund only if their loan sources deny the client's loan request and a loan for an equivalent or greater amount is later obtained from another lender. In addition to the advance fee, if the broker locates the loan money, the client usually pays a percentage of the total received at the time the loan becomes effective.

The fees a loan broker charges usually are high, but to the borrower, finding the money needed to save a business may be worth almost any price.

Sorry, Wrong Number

Many local Better Business Bureaus have conducted surveys of questionable loan activities in the advance fee loan business. Brokers were asked what kinds of services they offered; the amount, if any, of advance fee charged; the dollar volume of funds located for clients in a twelve-month period; and the main source – advance fees or percentages of located funds – of their income. Bureaus also asked for customer and banking references. In many cases brokers refused to reply, and follow-up calls found some broker phones disconnected. You should contact your local Better Business Bureau before doing business with a loan broker.

Variations on the Scheme

Complaint files at the local BBBs disclose a number of variations on advance fee loan schemes. In most fraudulent cases, a broker fee is paid and the broker drops out of sight, goes "out of business," or points out that the fine print on the signed contracts makes no guarantee of funding.

When a business seeks a refund of the advance fee because the broker has failed to provide an agreed-upon number of lender referrals, the broker may provide the names of potential lenders who in reality have little or no interest in lending the money, or the broker may employ any of a variety of excuses to withhold the refund.

In some of the most brazen yet successful schemes, brokers offer to provide contacts with potential sources of investment capital. Then, advance fee in hand, these con artists fulfill their obligations (at least under the letter of the law) by mailing lists containing the names and addresses of local banks, savings and loan associations, and other financial institutions.

Looking for money to expand, build, start, or save your business? Risk capital is available if you know where to look, without giving up much equity. Phone 222-333-4444 start the ball rolling. Act today.

Loans from private investors, regardless of credit history. From $5,000 to $10 Million. Confidential. Call toll free 1-800-123-1234.

Need money? Up to $10,000 available. Guaranteed financing. Bad credit OK; no collateral needed; confidential. Call us today at 1-900-ACT-FAST!

HOW TO PROTECT YOUR BUSINESS

If your business is seeking a commercial loan through a broker, the answers to certain questions can help you to distinguish the legitimate operations from the schemes. Ask that the following information be provided to you in writing at least three days before any contract is signed and three days before you pay any broker fees:

1. The name, address, and telephone number of the broker.

2. The length of time the broker has been in business.

3. The total number of contracts the broker has signed in the preceding twelve months.

4. The number of successful contracts brokered in the preceding twelve months.

5. The percent of the broker's income derived from advance fees.

6. A complete description of services offered by the broker.

7. A full description of the broker's refund policy, including the circumstances under which you would not obtain a full

refund of an advance fee, if no funding is received. Some contracts provide that, if a loan is not obtained, the advance fee be refunded "after accounting for expenses incurred in preparing the application." But the fraudulent loan broker may manage to compute those expenses so they just equal or slightly exceed the fee paid. If a contract contains such a clause, you should insist on a firm estimate of the nature of the expenses to be charged back and the anticipated total of those expenses.

It is a wise precaution to have the agreement reviewed by a trusted lending institution or by your attorney before signing.

Think Like a Banker

Even if, for one reason or another, your business is seeking a loan through a loan broker rather than a bank, you may find it worthwhile to compare the approach a bank loan officer would take with that of the broker you are considering.

The bank loan officer will first scrutinize your business, its financial condition, and the purpose of the loan. The bank in all likelihood will not want to become involved in the operation of your business, but it will want to be assured that you have done your homework and are qualified to operate the business. The only way the lender can receive these assurances is to consider a number of questions.

For example, if you are buying a business, the loan officer will want to know how much it will cost per month to keep the doors open, how much business you must do each month to generate that amount, and whether the previous owners did that much business. The lender will be interested in your contingency plans for emergencies. Are you creating a cash reserve? Can you reduce expenses? You will probably be cross-examined about the accuracy of your projections and monthly cash flow analysis.

The point is that any legitimate loan broker or financial loan officer will want accurate, clear-cut answers to questions about your business. The primary concern of a representative of a legitimate loan organization is to ascertain that the loan will be repaid promptly and that if it is defaulted on, some form of backup or collateral exists.

With this in mind, be cautious of:

- Loan brokers who pay little attention to potential risks.

- Brokers who attempt to discourage you from bringing in a lawyer or financial adviser to look more closely at the lending institution.

- Brokers who continually divert your inquiries by extolling your business prospects.

- A long list of references or satisfied customers who, for one reason or another, cannot be contacted and may not exist. Also, be wary of references who immediately give a good report, without taking the time to check their records. They could be accomplices paid to sit by the telephone and wait for calls like yours.

- Brokers who claim no form of collateral is needed beyond your good intentions.

- Brokers who claim "foreign money" is readily available at surprisingly reasonable rates.

- Brokers who list their offices as post office boxes or who have impressive sounding, possibly nonexistent addresses.

- Brokers who continually arrange meetings at hotels, airports, or restaurants, and who have no permanent base of operations that can be conveniently visited.

- Brokers who need money "up-front" to help operate their businesses. In any case, you should insist that advance money be placed in an escrow account.

Banks and savings and loan institutions may be more strict in their requirements and less likely to handle "problem loans" than typical loan brokers. Be careful, though, because alternative lenders can be much tougher to deal with if you cannot repay the loan as agreed.

Applying for an SBA Loan

If you have been turned down for a loan from a bank, you may be entitled to apply for assistance from the federal government's Small Business Administration (SBA). Your bank loan officer can help you to apply for an SBA loan guarantee or direct loan. If your application is approved, the SBA will guarantee a portion of your bank loan.

The SBA's General Business Loan Program can provide guarantees of up to 90 percent of the loan amount, up to $750,000. Loan terms and interest rates are negotiated between the lender and the borrower.

The SBA also has several specific programs designed to provide financial and advisory assistance to:

- Small businesses located in areas with high unemployment.

- Small businesses owned by socially and economically disadvantaged people, including women and minorities.

- Small businesses damaged by natural disasters, such as hurricanes, flooding, and earthquakes.

Shop Around

Even if your regular bank is not the selected source of funding, your banker usually will be willing to talk with you about your plans. His or her advice and referrals could be very useful.

If your banker cannot help you and you find that your business does not qualify for an SBA guarantee, you can shop around for other potential sources of funds by contacting organizations listed in the phone book under loans or financial services.

Your approach to obtaining a commercial loan should not be much different from shopping for the best deal on a house, appliance, or other major purchase. Speak with a wide variety of people, make certain all your questions are answered satisfactorily, and don't hesitate to seek outside professional advice.

The reputation that your potential loan broker has in the community can provide a good indication of his or her business conduct. Ask the opinions of business colleagues who have had similar needs, and don't be reluctant to ask the lender for a list of references and to check those references.

Be certain that you understand everything involved with the loan before you sign any documents. If in doubt, consult an attorney, accountant, or financial adviser.

Before you enter into an arrangement with a loan broker,

consider these questions:

☐ Have you explored all the alternatives to an advance fee loan broker?

☐ Is the broker using sources available to you directly?

☐ Is a distant lender more likely to assist you through a loan broker than traditional sources close to home – particularly if you already have been turned down by those local sources?

WHAT TO DO IF YOU ARE VICTIMIZED

If you believe you have been the victim of an advance fee loan scam, file both verbal and written complaints with the local branch of the FBI, listed in your telephone directory, and your local Better Business Bureau (see Appendix B). If any of the elements of the scheme, such as contracts or agreements, were sent through the U.S. mail, also contact your local U.S. Postal Service office and the Chief Postal Inspector, U.S. Postal Service (see Appendix A). It is important that you assemble and save all the documents involved in the transaction, along with names, addresses, telephone numbers, and other pertinent information.

The BBB and the FBI or the U.S. Postal Service can help you determine whether you indeed have been the victim of an illegal operation. If so, contact your attorney for advice and assistance in pursuing your case.

CHAPTER 5

Bankruptcy Fraud

 ## THE CASE OF
The Menacing Merchants

The new owners of a men's clothing store announce intentions of widening their selection and eventually expanding into a chain of clothing and accessories stores. Accomplishing their ambitious plans will require a large amount of capital, and so, they explain to suppliers, they must depart from the previous owner's policy of paying for all purchases within thirty days. With suppliers' cooperation, the expansion plans should quickly lead to bigger orders and increased profits for all.

The new owners also convince local bankers to provide secondary mortgage funds to augment their "working capital."

As new clothing and accessories orders begin to pour in, the owners place a few of each item on store shelves and secretly ship the remainder to a warehouse several hundred miles away. While some of the "working capital" is used to spruce up the store, most is quietly routed out of town.

With credit extended to the hilt, the owners spring the trap. Their store ostensibly is broken into and stripped of its merchandise. The police are summoned, an investigation ensues, several leads are followed, but the case eventually dead-ends. The store owners, it is disclosed, had no business insurance; they have no alternative but to file for bankruptcy.

Creditors wrangle over the few remaining worthwhile assets, and most are left with substantial losses. The owners assist in the final stages of bankruptcy, and several months later, slip out of town – to claim their secreted funds and quietly arrange for the sale of the stored merchandise.

How Bankruptcy Fraud Works

Spurred by a soft economy and heavy debt burdens, U.S. business failures climbed 20 percent, to 60,432 in 1990, up from 50,361 in 1989.* When personal bankruptcies are added in, the figure soars to more than 800,000 filings in the first half of 1991.** Many of the firms filing for bankruptcy-court protection are not "megacorporations" but rather small or medium-sized companies. And many economists predict that the situation will worsen before it improves.

The boom in business failures has proved a boon for con artists specializing in bankruptcy fraud. Prosecutions of bankruptcy fraud increased about 20 percent in the first half of 1991.** And while there are no solid figures on losses from this form of fraud, some authorities put the cost at about $1 billion annually. Hardest hit are small businesses that unknowingly sell goods on credit to swindlers.

In its simplest form, bankruptcy fraud involves the purchase of merchandise on credit, the surreptitious sale of the merchandise, concealment of the proceeds, and subsequent filing for bankruptcy. Historically, organized crime and individual con artists have carried out the majority of these schemes. Recently, however, a strong trend has developed in which formerly honest businesspeople, hoping to save something for themselves from the crumbling structure of their failing businesses, turn to fraud. These white-collar criminals have been known to operate from the highest levels of the corporate world, so no one today is above the scrutiny of law enforcement officials.

The federal bankruptcy laws, according to business and law enforcement officials, have created an environment that encourages bankruptcy fraud to flourish. Under the shelter of Chapter 11 of the federal bankruptcy code, the operator of a bankrupt company often can still conduct business, cleansed of debt, with creditors and bondholders left out in the cold. A 1978 change in the bankruptcy code allowed debtors to retain more of their possessions than ever before. As a result, some have found it more financially attractive to opt for bankruptcy

*Source: Dun & Bradstreet. Figures for 1990 are preliminary
**Source: Gannett Suburban Newspapers

than to work their way out of a financial crisis. And some businesspersons intending to file for bankruptcy take advantage of today's more lenient bankruptcy codes to actually improve their personal financial position.

A Variety of Schemes

The many ingenious variations on bankruptcy fraud include:

☐ **The creation of a bogus company.** A company is formed by simply depositing a moderate amount of money in a bank account to establish credit. Misleading balance sheets and income statements are prepared for the inspection of potential victims.

☐ **Company takeovers.** A business with financial problems, usually one that is well known in the community, is purchased with a minimal down payment. While the new owners might begin their operation by paying cash for small orders, the volume of orders quickly grows and a line of credit is established. The goods are sold at bargain prices or secretly moved to another location, and the business folds – thanks to "poor business practices," an overnight "robbery," fire damage, or some other "unexpected catastrophe."

☐ **Failed business.** The long-time owner of a legitimate firm sees bankruptcy as the best way out of a failing business. Buying, spending, and credit practices may be orchestrated to result in a profitable bankruptcy.

☐ **Bust-outs.** In this variation of the above three schemes, the proprietors do not file for bankruptcy – they leave town. While not literally a form of bankruptcy, a bust-out includes many of the elements of bankruptcy fraud.

HOW TO PROTECT YOUR BUSINESS

Be alert to these telltale signs of bankruptcy fraud:

● A sudden change in a business's management, particularly a change occurring without public notice.

- A business that lists only a post office box as its contact point.

- A business that uses an answering service.

- A customer whose credit balance begins to climb dramatically.

- A new customer that suddenly begins to place many orders on credit, or one that switches from paying cash to strictly credit.

- A new customer whose credit references either cannot be contacted or give a good report immediately, without looking at records. The unreachable references may not exist; their overeager counterparts may be parties to the scheme.

- Rush orders, particularly those of substantial numbers, from a new customer or from a business that previously has not placed orders in any great quantity.

- A business with a prestigious-sounding name or a name that is strikingly similar to that of a well-established and well-financed company.

If in doubt, remember that your Better Business Bureau (see Appendix B) can provide you with information on the reliability of a local business. While much of the information in BBB reports deals with customer experiences with the subject, the BBB also can provide data, if available, on company principals, government actions, and prior bankruptcy proceedings.

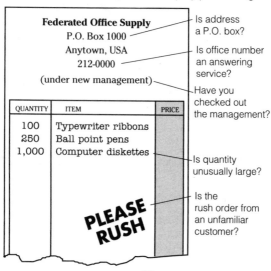

Federated Office Supply
P.O. Box 1000 — Is address a P.O. box?
Anytown, USA
212-0000 — Is office number an answering service?
(under new management) — Have you checked out the management?

QUANTITY	ITEM	PRICE
100	Typewriter ribbons	
250	Ball point pens	
1,000	Computer diskettes	— Is quantity unusually large?

PLEASE RUSH — Is the rush order from an unfamiliar customer?

WHAT TO DO IF YOU ARE VICTIMIZED

Because many of the signs of an impending bankruptcy fraud are also commonplace among legitimate enterprises merely experiencing slow business periods, bankruptcy fraud usually goes undetected until it is too late.

If an occurrence of those warning signs described on pages 61 and 62 makes you believe that a bankruptcy fraud is imminent, curtail further transactions with the suspect business, stop deliveries of goods, prevent further credit allowances, and state clearly that payment is overdue and is expected without delay.

It is, of course, important that you not spread possibly false and damaging rumors. However, if you strongly suspect foul play, contact the local offices of the FBI and the office of your local district attorney, both of which should be listed in your telephone directory. Be prepared to provide details of your business arrangements with the suspect business and your reasons for suspecting fraud. A number of violations of the law could come into play in a bankruptcy fraud, including, among others, the illegal falsification of business records, the defrauding of secured creditors, fraud in insolvency, the public issuance of false financial statements, and the receipt of deposits in a failing financial institution.

CHAPTER 6

Business Opportunity and Investment Schemes

THE CASE OF
Bitter Sweets

A worker dissatisfied with his salary and his nine to five routine comes across a magazine ad offering an opportunity to enter the "rapidly expanding, lucrative vending machine business." If managed properly, the ad proclaims, this business can lead the investor "to earn unlimited income by working the hours you want to work." For an initial investment of $1,995, the applicant will receive complete ownership of his own equipment, plus the guarantee of a high-traffic location requiring minimal servicing. The ad's glowing testimonials from investors who have earned thousands of dollars in their spare time clinch the matter – the disgruntled worker, with high hopes for a profitable future, sends in a check for $1,995.

The vending machine that eventually arrives is a cheaply made candy dispenser, complete with an introductory supply of off-brand candy. Additional candy supplies are available only from the vending machine company. The "high-traffic" location turns out to be a nearby roadside rest stop where several other vending machines offer similar products.

During his first six months of operation, the worker's average monthly profit is $25 – or, considering transportation costs, supplies, and the time involved in servicing the machine, just over $2 for each hour worked.

When the vending machine breaks down, the owner finds that its warranty has expired and repairs will cost $150. He attempts to repair the machine himself and, failing that, throws it in his basement, where it will become a permanent, unpleasant reminder of his bad investment.

Business Opportunities Abound

The opportunity to "be your own boss," "work your own hours," and earn "unlimited amounts of money" attracts thousands of Americans each year. And, of course, many business opportunity offers are both legitimate and profitable. According to the International Franchise Association, business format franchises (restaurants, retail stores, printing services) and product and trade name franchises (auto dealerships, gas stations) accounted for a total of $714.6 billion in 1990, or one-third of all U.S. retail sales. Unfortunately, as independent business opportunities expand, a growing number of con artists move in, with the intent of making it difficult for those wishing to enter the field to distinguish the bona fide opportunities from the schemes. In fact, fraudulent work-at-home "opportunities" were the second most frequently encountered scheme reported to Better Business Bureaus in early 1991.

The FTC (Federal Trade Commission), which regulates some of the activities of independent businesses, notes that while it is impossible to estimate the number of people defrauded by business opportunity schemes, annual losses may run into the billions of dollars. One reason statistics are hard to come by is that the variety of schemes seems virtually limitless. Among the most common are schemes practiced in the areas of:

- Franchising

- Vending machines

- Mail-order businesses

- Multilevel marketing

- Land development

- Invention marketing

- Work-at-home enterprises

- Telemarketing investments (see pages 81 to 83)

Inside the Schemes

Franchising Fraud

Franchising has become one of the most popular ways for Americans to start their own businesses. Through franchising, a company achieves rapid and effective distribution of its products or services by sharing, through contractual agreement, its economic means and the possibility for profits with independent businesspeople. The franchisor may provide only a trademark and method of doing business, or a product or entire line of products.

While the majority of franchisors are legitimate, a number of them operate under false pretenses. In these cases, the victim may be subjected to a fast-paced, high-pressure sales pitch – complete with fictitious sales projections, testimonials, and slick promotional brochures – in which he or she is urged to act immediately to take advantage of a "ground floor" opportunity. After the sale has been completed and money collected, any of a number of possible scenarios may ensue:

☐ The sales representative – and the company represented – disappear with the investment.

☐ The franchisor goes out of business.

☐ Products or services turn out to be inferior, overpriced, or unmarketable.

☐ The franchise location is poorly trafficked.

☐ The specialized training promised by the franchisor is insufficient or nonexistent.

☐ Field support from the franchisor is inadequate.

☐ Advertising or promotions promised by the franchisor are inadequate or nonexistent.

☐ Whatever the reason, the investor duped into purchasing a business franchise under false pretenses sees plans for success fall to pieces.

Vending Machine Fraud

Like franchising frauds, vending machine frauds are aimed at investors hoping to tap a time-tested, nationally recognized consumer market. The victim of this type of scheme usually relies on the vending company to select the product, equipment, and optimal location. Often, the outcome is similar to the scenarios listed above. Additional factors in the failure of fraudulently sold businesses include:

- Machines placed in arcades or other locations where numerous other machines offer similar or better products.

- Machines that do not work properly.

- Vending supplies that cannot be sold at a reasonable profit.

- Machines that require servicing and refilling far more time-consuming than anticipated.

Mail-order Business Scams

In 1990, mail-order sales topped two hundred billion dollars. It is not surprising that many mail-order entrepreneurs have become wealthy by offering to help others tap into this vast and lucrative market. Unfortunately, some of these seemingly honest business brokers are actually in the business of conning luckless individuals out of hard-earned start-up capital, with the consequent costs of time and effort wasted in working toward an unattainable goal.

Mail-order business opportunities commonly are offered through advertisements in newspapers, magazines, and business journals. The ads may promise would-be entrepreneurs the chance to supplement their income by selling products through the mail. Huge returns, with virtually no expense or labor, are promised. But in reality, the products offered by the promoter, either directly or through unnamed suppliers, are shoddy, stale, and of dubious sales appeal. Of equally dubious value are the instructions, catalogs, mailing lists, and advice some promoters provide.

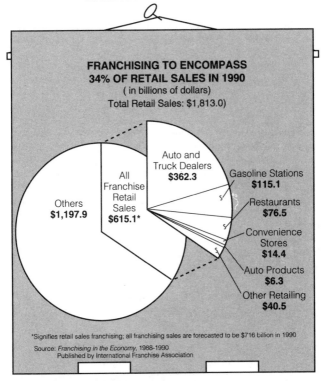

**FRANCHISING TO ENCOMPASS
34% OF RETAIL SALES IN 1990**
(in billions of dollars)
Total Retail Sales: $1,813.0)

Auto and
Truck Dealers
$362.3

Gasoline Stations
$115.1

All
Franchise
Retail
Sales
$615.1*

Restaurants
$76.5

Others
$1,197.9

Convenience
Stores
$14.4

Auto Products
$6.3

Other Retailing
$40.5

*Signifies retail sales franchising; all franchising sales are forecasted to be $716 billion in 1990

Source: *Franchising in the Economy*, 1988-1990
Published by International Franchise Association

Multilevel Marketing Schemes

A legitimate form of retailing, multilevel marketing is a system in which independent businesspeople, often called distributors, sell the products or services of a multilevel marketing company to small businesses or consumers. Most sales are made in customers' homes, and distributors set their own hours, with earning levels dependent upon the extent of their efforts and sales ability.

Most multilevel marketing companies encourage distributors to build and manage their own sales forces by recruiting, training, supplying, and motivating others to sell the products or services. Distributors who recruit other distributors are rewarded with a percentage based on the sales of their entire sales force.

Legitimate multilevel marketing companies stress that there is no easy path to riches – that success can come only through consistent dedication and hard work.

Pyramid schemes, also known as "chain letter" schemes, are illegal variations of the multilevel marketing system. The emphasis in a pyramid scheme is on the quick profits to be earned by recruiting others, who in turn will recruit others, and so on – with each new recruit paying a specified sum that goes to those higher up in the chain. Although promotional literature or sales pitches may present this as a business opportunity, the merchandise or service to be sold is largely ignored and, in fact, there may be little potential for actually making sales.

In some pyramid schemes, there *is* no product or service, or the product exists only in token form to show prospects that the promoter is a member of the "sales team." New recruits are paid commissions or bonuses for signing up other investors, who also receive token products. Scant mention is made of the fact that the ever-increasing number of participants, all attempting to recoup their investments by recruiting from the ever-

TOTAL SALES /ALL FRANCHISING 1980-1990

$ billions

*estimated figures

Source: *Franchising in the Economy, 1988-1990*
Published by International Franchise Association

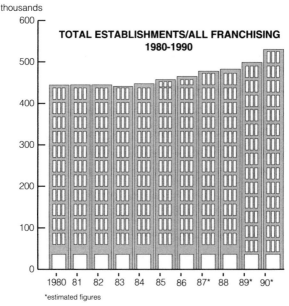

Source: *Franchising in the Economy, 1988-1990*
Published by International Franchise Association

decreasing ranks of potential investors in a given area, will quickly result in market saturation.

Consider the results if one person recruited six distributors, each of whom in turn recruited six others, and carry the process through nine steps as follows:

	1
1	6
2	36
3	216
4	1,296
5	7,776
6	46,656
7	279,936
8	1,679,616
9	10,077,696

At more than ten million people for every nine steps in the distribution program, the distributors soon would be recruiting one another. In order for everyone to profit in a pyramid scheme, there would have to be a never-ending supply of potential (and willing) participants. Obviously, there isn't. When the supply runs out, the pyramid collapses and most participants lose their investment.

Land Development Fraud

Many business owners, investors, and consumers believe that land is always a good investment. Land fraud artists capitalize on that belief with schemes to sell or lease properties that have little or no tangible value.

Consumers are most frequently targeted by schemes to sell property ostensibly located in resort areas or urban developments that in reality is undesirable or unsuitable for reasonable use. Businesses may be duped into investing in dilapidated inner-city business districts or into leasing space in nonexistent, poorly situated, improperly financed, or inadequately insured business office buildings, co-ops, or condominiums.

Land fraud con artists usually employ high-pressure sales tactics. Their printed literature, usually sent through the mail, and their verbal sales pitches, often delivered by phone, may contain glittering generalities about the benefits of owning property in the bustling inner city or in sunny resort locales. More specific, informative details are frequently difficult to come by.

Invention Marketing Fraud

Once you've invented the better mousetrap, how do you get it to market? Many legitimate invention marketing firms are in the business of helping investors with that problem; other fraudulent firms concentrate on collecting their victims' money while doing little or nothing to move their inventions to market.

Fraudulent firms may advertise in the same scientific and business journals, magazines, and news publications as their legitimate counterparts. The illegal operations may charge various up-front fees for nonexistent services. They may promise to research the uniqueness of an invention, survey its marketability, obtain a patent, and produce and market the product. Con artists have been known to swindle inventors out of thousands of dollars by claiming they are developing a prototype or arranging for the mass production of an invention. But what these firms do best is swindle their unsuspecting victims by preying on vanity, emotions, hopes, and inexperience.

Work-at-home Schemes

Computers, products made at home, and services that can be offered from an office at home are creating new opportunities for individuals hoping to go into business for themselves by working from their homes. Yet the increasing interest in these cottage industries has its negative side. Today, a growing number of Americans are falling victim to work-at-home schemes. Federal law enforcement agencies explain that total losses by these victims are almost impossible to estimate. Most losses are under $100 and are never reported to authorities because victims wish to avoid the embarrassment or bother involved in filing a complaint.

Victims of work-at-home schemes usually are hooked through newspaper advertisements. A typical ad might offer to show the respondent how to "earn $100 a week by addressing envelopes in your spare time at home." Unsuspecting victims who mail their $19.95 for details are sent instructions on how to write and place similar ads in their own local newspapers.

Other more complex, costlier schemes might offer to set up the respondent in a full-fledged business enterprise. If you were to respond, you might be trained to produce, for example, a certain mechanical or electronic device that supposedly is part of a larger mechanism to be assembled by the mail-order company. The company guarantees it will purchase your products, and after investing several thousand dollars in training, equipment, and supplies, you begin turning out the devices and shipping them to the company. The devices are returned with a letter explaining that their quality is below standards. The small print in your signed contract explains that the mail-order firm has the option of rejecting products it considers unacceptable – and what it considers acceptable turns out to be beyond your reach.

HOW TO PROTECT YOUR BUSINESS

By the time you realize you have been the victim of a business opportunity fraud, it usually is too late. You have invested your money and the con artists most likely have closed up operations and moved on. Even if you are fortunate enough to catch the swindlers in the act, prosecution may prove difficult or impossible. And if you are able to prosecute and win your case, there is no guarantee you will recover any of the money you invested.

Therefore, precaution is your best line of defense.

1. **Find out as much as possible about the reliability of the firm offering the business opportunity.**

   ☐ Ask for financial statements for the past three years and verify that they have been audited by a reputable firm. Financial statements should include full details on operating revenues and source of revenues, as well as a profit and loss statement.

   ☐ Ask for evidence or research to support claims of growth potential and profitability, and have an accountant look it over.

   ☐ Ask for and check business, bank, and client references. Be wary if references seem to respond too quickly and eagerly; they may be accomplices waiting for such calls.

   ☐ Find out how long the firm has been in business and ask for information on its litigation record. Look for lawsuits, bankruptcy proceedings, or charges of embezzlement, fraud, or unfair or deceptive practices.

   ☐ If the business opportunity involves door-to-door sales, find out if the firm is a member of the Direct Selling Association (see Appendix A).

   ☐ Remember that firms offering legitimate business opportunities are interested in answering your questions fully. If a firm cannot or will not answer key questions, you would be wise to avoid further involvement.

2. **Before you enter into a business arrangement, make certain you fully understand the responsibilities of all parties.** Have your attorney or accountant go over the details of the agreement.

In Franchising and Sales Opportunities

Be aware of the fact that the Federal Trade Commission (FTC) requires franchisors to provide certain information at the earlier of either the first personal meeting to discuss a franchise purchase with the potential investor or no later than ten business days before the investor signs a franchise or related agreement or pays any money in connection with the purchase. This information includes identifying information about the franchisor, background information on the business and its officers, and substantial details on how the franchise arrangement is to work and what restrictions, such as geographical boundaries to territories or conditions on the right to sell or transfer ownership, are to be placed on either party.

In the case of business opportunities that appear to guarantee "territorial rights," insist on a written explanation of the restrictions to be imposed upon you or upon potential competitors who also buy into the business.

In Invention Marketing

The FTC recommends that inventors shop for a marketing firm just as they would any major service provider. Ask for and contact references, including organizations and institutions with which the firm has dealt and other inventors who have been successfully marketed. Ask for a written curriculum vitae detailing academic and career achievements on each of the principals. Insist on a written explanation of fees and services.

The U.S. Patent Office points out that inventors can do some of the initial legwork themselves. A public patent search facility is located at 2021 Jefferson Davis Highway, Arlington, Virginia. The Patent Office, which in 1990 issued nearly ninety-seven thousand patents, provides this facility so that individuals can determine whether patents have been issued for products or services similar to their inventions. The Patent Office also publishes a booklet, "General Information Concerning Patents," containing a step-by-step guide to the patent process. In addition, you can contact the Commissioner of Patents and Trademarks, Washington, D.C. 20231, for a list of registered patent attorneys in your geographical area.

In General

For general information about possibly fraudulent business practices in your area, contact your state attorney general's office, listed under state government in most telephone directories.

3. **The actions and qualifications of sales agents may provide indications of the reliability of the firms they represent.**

   ☐ Be wary of sales agents who emphasize the profitability of recruiting others into the business rather than making sales and providing exceptional service.

   ☐ Be wary of sales agents who offer you "free" merchandise as an inducement to buy.

   ☐ Check the qualifications of sales agents or dealers. Often the easiest way to do this is by contacting the associations that license agents in their area of specialty. For example, agents selling land or property must possess a real estate license issued by the state's real estate commission. That commission can tell you whether the agent is certified and has obtained the required training.

4. **Be on the alert for the following signs of potentially fraudulent activity.**

   ☐ Be wary of business opportunities that promise quick or unusually high returns on "once-in-a-lifetime" investments. Ask yourself what might be behind such "rare and generous" offers.

☐ Be skeptical of "private sales" or offerings, particularly those in which substantial discounts are offered on so-called list prices.

☐ Don't be taken in by impressive-sounding company names or addresses.

☐ Be particularly cautious about doing business with firms located outside the U.S. It may become difficult or even impossible to trace and recover your money.

☐ Look closely at the quality of printed documents. Deeds, securities, guarantees, or other supposedly official documents may be counterfeits, and an unprofessional printing job could be the tip-off.

☐ Don't be fooled by initial easily obtained returns on your investment. A smooth con artist may use your investment to pay these returns, in order to entice you to invest even more heavily.

5. **Investigate before you invest.**

☐ Before buying or investing in an enterprise, product, or property, check with others in similar businesses to see if the price quoted is reasonable.

☐ Before buying into a sales or mail-order business, look carefully at the quality of the product or service, its potential market, your profit margin, and the reliability and background of the mail-order company.

☐ Before doing business with a firm, contact your local Better Business Bureau (see Appendix B) for a reliability report.

WHAT TO DO IF YOU ARE VICTIMIZED

Business opportunity schemes are often carefully constructed to conform to the letter of the law. Or they may operate in a gray area of the law where rulings generally fall in their favor.

Whatever the case, if you believe you have been the victim of a business opportunity scheme, you should:

1. Contact your local police department.

2. Stop payment on checks in transit.

3. Contact the state or federal agencies that oversee activities in your area of concern and provide them with full details, in writing, of the fraud. For example, if victimized in a franchising scheme that involved documents sent through the U.S. mail, you would send complete details to the FTC and the Chief Postal Inspector, U.S. Postal Service. Addresses and phone numbers for these and other agencies can be found in Appendix A.

4. Call your local Better Business Bureau (see Appendix B), and send the Bureau copies of the material going to the federal or state agency.

While it is often difficult, if not impossible, to recoup losses suffered in a fraudulent business opportunity scheme, your efforts in contacting and informing the appropriate authorities may help to prevent others from being victimized.

CHAPTER 7

Telemarketing Crimes

THE CASE OF
The Vanishing Vendor

The business manager of a small chain of real estate offices receives a call from the regional sales rep of an advertising specialty product supplier. "For a limited time only," high-quality nickel-plated pens, custom-imprinted with the customer's name and phone number, are available at a bargain price. What clinches the sale is the special bonus prize awarded for first-time orders of $1,000 or more – a valuable personal computer.

The order is placed for two thousand pens at fifty cents each. Two weeks later the cartons arrive COD – including one very large box marked "Handle with Care." The business manager, troubled by the extra $150 added to the invoice to cover shipping, handling, insurance, and a "prize redemption fee," makes a mental note to take the matter up with the supplier. After writing out a check, as instructed, to the U.S. Postal Service and stamping it with the signature of the company president, she directs that the cartons of pens be placed in the storeroom and the large box holding the personal computer taken to her office. There she discovers to her dismay that the bulky carton contains nothing but volumes of shredded newspaper plus a rather small box. Inside the box is a very ordinary-looking handheld calculator. Red-faced, she pries open a carton of pens. A glance is enough to reveal that they are of inferior quality.

In two angry telephone calls to the sales rep, the business manager gets the runaround; on the third call, she gets a recorded message that the number is no longer in service. The address on the shipping invoice is a post office box. Her bank informs her that it's impossible to stop payment on a check made out to the U.S. Postal Service. And a belated survey of advertising specialty suppliers reveals that imprinted plastic pens are available locally at half the price paid to the fraudulent vendor.

Typical Telemarketing Scams

Many of the schemes, scams, and frauds covered in this book are perpetrated by phone. Office supply schemes, phony invoice schemes, fraudulent charitable solicitations – all involve at least an initial telephone contact to set the scam in motion. In this chapter we'll focus on several other major telemarketing ripoffs that the BBB and federal investigators are discovering in the con artist's bag of tricks for the 1990s.

Accurate figures for the totals lost by businesses and consumers to telemarketing schemes are impossible to come by, since many of these frauds go unreported due to the victim's embarrassment or sense of futility. The Federal Trade Commission estimates that telemarketing scam artists take in some one billion dollars each year. Others put the figure much higher – as high as ten billion dollars annually, says the North American Securities Administrators Association, the organization of state officials who administer and enforce the securities laws.

The telescam artists raking in those billions are cashing in on the success of the fast-growing legitimate telemarketing industry. With over $201 billion in products and services sold by phone in 1989, telemarketing has become an extremely popular way to contact great numbers of potential customers quickly and easily in an effort to sell a variety of products and services. Home improvements, security systems, insurance policies, business supplies, and newspaper and magazine subscriptions are just a few of the products often sold by phone. But as telephone marketing has flourished as a legitimate method of selling, it also has become a popular means of defrauding consumers and businesses. Con artists who work the phones constantly come up with new scams, from fraudulent health care promotions featuring the latest headline-grabbing drug or therapy to investment-related frauds that take advantage of fluctuations in the economy and current investment fads.

With few exceptions, illicit telemarketers are agents of the kinds of boiler room and "WATS-line" operations described on pages 20 to 22. These long-distance hustlers operate from crowded back offices, with a dozen or more salespeople crammed in a room, each placing hundreds of calls a day to out-of-state or overseas contacts. Their victims' names come from phone directories or from "sucker lists" acquired from other boiler room operations. No one knows how many boiler rooms are in operation today, but the number is surely in the thousands. Many are located in southern California, the Southwest, and Florida, with an increasing number moving operations offshore, beyond the reach of U.S. law enforcement.

No one is beyond the reach of these smooth-talking, persuasive, persistent salespeople and their carefully scripted pitches. Every type of business and professional office is a potential target, and even highly sophisticated businesspeople have been swindled. However, there are steps you can take to protect yourself from telemarketing fraud. The first step is to educate yourself and your employees about the workings of the most common telemarketing scams, which include:

- Office supply schemes, phony invoice schemes, and fraudulent charitable solicitations, covered in chapters one, two, and three

- Telemarketing investment scams

- Advertising specialty product promotions

- 900-number ripoffs

- PBX fraud

- Teleblackmail

Telemarketing Investment Scams

Because of the ease of establishing fraudulent operations and the popularity of telephone marketing, there has been a dramatic increase in recent years in the incidence of investment fraud perpetrated by phone. In fact, roughly three-quarters of the investment scams investigated by the Federal Trade Commission (FTC) involve telephone sales.

Investments sold by telescam artists have included coins, gemstones, artwork, oil and gas leases, precious metals such as gold and silver, and strategic metals such as chromium. Also common are telemarketing frauds involving securities and commodity futures investments and blind pool penny stocks. Like other fraudulent telemarketing operations, investment telescams usually are carried out by boiler room operators, who may target those who have indicated an interest in other investments by responding to a newspaper ad or filling out an information request card. Another common target is the individual already victimized by an earlier scam – the con artist knows that someone who has been defrauded once may be vulnerable to a second scam promising to make up for previous losses.

Telescam operators often find a receptive audience among the millions of investors who are accustomed to conducting legitimate stock and bond transactions through their brokers by phone. These persuasive operators often weave together half-truths and facts in a pitch that guarantees large profits and low risk. They may claim that the prospect has been specially selected to participate in an unusual investment opportunity. Often they will urge that the victim pay money immediately to "get in on the deal," and they may quote phony statistics to demonstrate the need for fast action. A messenger may even be dispatched to pick up funds before the target has had a chance to investigate or reconsider.

Here's how a few of the more common telemarketing investment scams work:

☐ In an **art print scam,** an investor hoping to cash in on the rising value of limited edition prints by popular artists finds that he or she is actually in possession of counterfeits. Overwhelmed by the feverish sales pitch of a boiler room operator purportedly calling from an art gallery – a pitch that may include the claim that the artist's health is failing and the value of the artist's work about to skyrocket – customers have paid thousands of dollars for nearly worthless photo-mechanical reproductions.

☐ In **bank-financed precious metals schemes,** investors put down 20 percent or more toward the purchase of gold or silver and the promoter arranges for bank financing of the balance of the purchase, using the precious metal as collateral. The promise is that the investor will make huge profits when the price of gold or silver rises. In reality, the investor ends up losing most or all of the down payment – the price would have to soar an unlikely 20 percent or more to make up for commissions, dealer markups, finance charges, and other stiff fees.

☐ In **securities and commodity futures investment,** most criminal activities center around the sale of misrepresented properties. Examples include the sale of counterfeit or stolen securities, schemes that rely on the deceitful practices of traders or employees "inside" stock and bond clearinghouses, and international schemes involving the sale of securities in nonexistent foreign companies. Fraudulent commodity sales operations often use glossy brochures touting trading "successes." They may adopt a legitimate-sounding name and an impressive mailing address that in reality is nothing more than a mail drop or rented back office. Most of these questionable operations are not members of legitimate exchanges and are not registered with any regulatory agency, even though, in most instances, registration with a regulatory body such as the Commodity Futures Trading Commission or the National Futures Association is mandatory for firms dealing with customers in commodity futures or options transactions.

☐ In **blind pool penny stock scams,** telephone hucksters often pass themselves off as brokers with inside information on a hot new stock issue. Typically, the blind pool prospectus contains no indication of exactly where or how the money invested will be put to work, if at all. The investor "goes in blind," relying on the promoter's exaggerated claims of large returns for a small investment. The one who makes the quick and easy profits, however, usually is not the investor but the promoter. In a typical scam, the promoting company's officers, brokers, and other insiders purchase stock at a fraction of what the public pays. Once boiler room sales have driven up the price, the promoters sell out at a fat profit, the stock prices collapses, and investors are left holding the bag.

☐ In **foreign bank investment scams,** telemarketing con artists extol the benefits of investing in loans, CDs, insurance, currency speculation programs, and other financial offerings of foreign banks. False claims are made regarding the high returns guaranteed from such investments. Profits are anything but guaranteed. In most cases, the investor's money goes no farther than the promoter's pocket.

Advertising Specialty Product Promotions

Advertising specialty products – pens, calendars, key tags, T-shirts, and other items imprinted with a company's name, logo, and/or advertising message – can be effective promotional tools. Unfortunately, these products also have proven to be an effective tool in the hands of the telemarketing con artist. The fraudulent phone sale of advertising specialty products often is coupled with the promise of a free gift or prize, such as a personal computer, a VCR, or an exotic vacation, as an incentive to order. In fact, these "gifts" are of far less value than represented. The personal computer may turn out to be a handheld calculator and the "free" vacation could end up costing thousands of dollars in transportation or hotel fees. Often a catch such as a "redemption charge," shipping and handling fee, insurance fee, or other hidden cost is tacked on to the invoice, with the fee exceeding the value of the prize. Further, the advertising specialty products ordered may be of inferior quality and higher price than similar merchandise available from local vendors.

900-Number Ripoffs

Consumers and businesses alike have become targets of a new telemarketing scam involving 900-numbers. Callers to telephone numbers with prefixes such as 900, 976, and 540 may be charged anywhere from fifty cents a minute to fifty dollars a call. Typical scams have involved TV ads and recorded phone messages promising callers services such as:

- **Real estate or job listings.** Callers usually end up paying to listen to a recording of listings taken from local newspapers or other publicly available sources.

- A **"gold" credit card.** Often these so-called gold cards can be used only to buy overpriced merchandise from the promoter's catalog – and there may even be an extra charge for obtaining the catalog.

- A **bank credit card,** available "regardless of credit history." All the caller usually receives is a list of banks offering low-interest or secured credit cards. (To qualify for a secured card, a consumer must open and maintain a savings account, which is used as collateral for the card's line of credit.) The lists the caller receives, usually for a very high price, often can be obtained at far less cost through financial magazines, newspapers, or legitimate consumer credit organizations. In another typical scam, the callee may be sent a "how-to kit" of virtually worthless generic information on reestablishing credit.

- **Bank loans.** Again, the caller usually receives nothing but a list of lenders or a generic information package on applying for a loan.

Although some states require 900-number ads to disclose per-minute or per-call charges, that requirement may not apply to calls below a specified threshold, and some promoters ignore the legal requirements entirely. Further, many 900-number scam operators hike their profits by putting callers on hold or otherwise prolonging the call to multiply their per-minute charges. Although consumers responding to credit ads are the most common victims of 900-number scams, businesses have found thousands of dollars charged to their phone bills when employees have been targeted with prerecorded phone messages promising that a "gold" card or some other desirable service is just a phone call away.

PBX Fraud

A growing number of businesses are falling victim to a new form of telemarketing fraud perpetrated through their corporate switchboards, known as private branch exchanges, or PBXs. PBX fraud operators use a variety of means to obtain the two numbers needed to make use of a PBX's remote access capability: the 800-number or seven- or ten-digit telephone number assigned to the Remote Access Unit or Direct Inward System Access feature of the PBX, and the password or authorization code employees must use when away from the office to place calls through the switchboard. Some listen in on employees using public pay phones, others search a company's garbage dumpsters, and still others use a computer to try thousands of numerical combinations in search of working codes. Once in possession of those access numbers, the telescam artists can place hundreds of calls anywhere in the world, all charged to the company's bill. Some scam operators sell the access codes they obtain, thus expanding their profits and multiplying the victim's losses, which in the case of large corporations can run into hundreds of thousands of dollars.

PBX fraud operators can be nearly impossible to track down. Some use a technique known as looping, in which calls are placed using two different PBXs, to evade detection. And often, by the time the unauthorized charges appear on a victim's bill, the PBX fraud operator has moved on to a new location and a new crop of corporate victims.

Teleblackmail

In a twist on the office supply telemarketing scheme (see chapter one), some scam operators have swindled businesses out of thousands of dollars by turning a telescam into teleblackmail. Typically, boiler room operators talk unsuspecting victims into purchasing off-brand office supplies. Once several orders have been placed and paid for, the operator tells the victim that, as a valued customer, he or she is entitled to receive a free gift, such as a tape recorder or VCR. When the victim later refuses to place further orders or to pay invoices for goods never ordered or received, the scammer threatens to inform higher-ups at the company that the employee accepted gifts in exchange for the orders. In one startling case uncovered in 1988, a school district's business manager paid out more than two million dollars over the course of six years to a teleblackmailer, in an elaborate scam that began with the "gift" of a pocket tape recorder.

■ HOW TO PROTECT YOUR BUSINESS ■

Awareness is your best defense against any telemarketing scam. When you receive a telephone sales call, find out who is calling, ask the caller to mail further information if you are interested, interrupt and say you are not interested if that's the case, and ask unwelcome callers to take your name off their list.

Remember that it is always your option to hang up when called by a stranger, as it is your choice to return and refuse payment for any unordered merchandise you receive.

It is critical to train your employees on the proper handling of telephone sales calls, and to make certain that untrained employees are instructed not to confirm telephone orders or give suspect callers information such as office equipment model numbers or the names of key employees. Another useful precaution is to keep up-to-date supplier lists by the phones for employees to double-check when vendors call.

When you did not originate a phone contact and are not familiar with the caller, be extremely cautious about supplying your credit card number. Also be wary if a caller urges that a decision concerning an investment or purchase be made immediately. Be suspicious of offers of free merchandise or prizes. Finally, review the tips given in earlier chapters for guarding against office supply schemes, phony invoice schemes, and fraudulent charitable solicitations, and make certain that you and your employees are aware of the specific precautions that can be taken to avoid scams in the following areas:

Telemarketing investment scams. When you receive telephone calls offering any form of investment opportunity, whether unsolicited or in answer to a request for information, keep these precautions in mind:

1. Be particularly skeptical of unsolicited calls, particularly from out-of-state salespeople.

2. Do not be high-pressured into buying. A warning that you must buy now or forever lose the opportunity should alert you to the possibility of fraud.

3. A red flag should go up warning you of fraud if the caller claims that the investment is risk-free, or that you can double your money or even expect a high return within a short time. Also be suspicious of testimonials, which are easily fabricated, and claims of "inside information."

4. Only put your money in investment opportunities you know something about. Get all the information you can about the company and then verify the data. Ask for a prospectus,

make sure you completely understand all its details, and check it with your attorney, stockbroker, or other reliable consultant.

5. Check the company's status and reputation with your local Better Business Bureau (see Appendix B) and the appropriate agencies and organizations. If, for example, you have questions about securities dealings, you should contact your state securities administrator, listed in your telephone directory, and the U.S. Securities and Exchange Commissions (SEC) Office of Consumer Affairs, or your regional SEC office. In questions involving commodity futures, contact the Commodity Futures Trading Commission (CFTC) or your regional CFTC office. You may also contact the National Futures Association, a self-regulatory organization in which membership is mandatory for any firm involved in commodity sales. Addresses and phone numbers of these and other organizations can be found in Appendix A.

6. If in any doubt, make no promises or commitments, no matter how tentative.

Advertising specialty product promotions. Before placing an order with an advertising specialty product supplier selling products by phone:

1. Check out the supplier with your local BBB.

2. Ask for the company's street address and phone number. When you call back, a person – not a recording or answering machine – should answer.

3. Compare prices for similar merchandise from local suppliers, and ask the caller for a sample of imprinted goods.

4. Be cautious of "one-time-only" offers requiring an immediate decision, especially when you are requested to give your credit card number over the phone.

5. Consider accepting the offer only if you are interested in the products for sale, not because you are tempted by a prize or "free" gift.

6. Be aware that the law covering Collect on Delivery shipments was changed in 1987 to allow recipients of COD packages to pay the charges with a check made payable to the sender

rather than to the U.S. Postal Service. That enables you to stop payment on your check if you think the goods you receive were misrepresented.

900-number ripoffs. Your best defense against excessive 900-number charges is to establish a firm policy regarding office phone use and make certain employees are aware of it. Employees should be briefed on the 900-number scam and reminded not to confuse 900-numbers with toll-free 800-numbers and to make certain they know what a 900-number call will cost before dialing. It is possible to adjust telephone systems so that outgoing 900-number calls cannot be made.

PBX fraud. Many long-distance carriers have begun working with corporate clients to help them combat PBX fraud. MCI Communications Corporation recommends that companies take these steps:

1. Learn all you can from the vendor who sold or services your PBX about the capabilities of the equipment, including its fraud defense features.

2. Delete all authorization codes programmed into the PBX for testing or service, and change active PBX codes frequently.

3. Limit PBX access to only employees who really need it, and make sure those employees understand the need to keep authorization codes confidential.

4. Use randomly selected authorization codes, not numbers based on personal information such as social security numbers.

5. Watch out for telescammers who misrepresent themselves to learn more about your phone system.

6. Block the PBX from making international calls if employees have little need to phone overseas, and consider cutting off remote access during nonbusiness hours.

7. Try these techniques for foiling hackers who program their computers to make multiple calls to your 800-number in order to figure out your authorization code:

   • Use a nonpublished 800-number for the Remote Access Unit.

- Use the longest authorization code your equipment will accept.

- Do not use a steady tone as the prompt for inputting the authorization code – use a voice recording instead or no prompt at all.

- Program your PBX to wait at least five rings before responding, and to cut off or reroute calls when an incorrect authorization code is entered.

WHAT TO DO IF YOU ARE VICTIMIZED

By the time you realize you have been the victim of a tele-marketing fraud, it is usually too late. Your money is gone, along with the telescammer, and you may be left with inferi-or merchandise, a worthless "prize," valueless stock ... or nothing at all.

Boiler room operators are particularly hard to track down and prosecute. They usually target out-of-state victims to avoid detection by local law enforcement authorities, and even when authorities are alerted to locally operated scams, the crooks often simply slip across state lines, change their names, and start operations again. Even when apprehended, these swindlers often get off lightly because of the small amounts involved in the individual swindles and because of the lack of legislation directed at these kinds of frauds.

Congressional legislation may remedy the major tele-marketing abuses – by giving states the authority to pursue telemarketing fraud cases in federal courts, making it illegal to solicit new credit card accounts unless authorized by a national credit card company or its affiliates, preventing credit laundering (see page 128), regulating 900-numbers, and requiring telemarketers to be bonded. In the meantime, some states and counties have enacted legislation specifically relat-ing to telemarketing operators. For example, in Florida tele-phone solicitors must identify the purpose of their call within thirty seconds and may not attempt to call people with unlisted numbers. A tough new California law requires telemarketers to meet strict licensing requirements. Further, in 1987 the Federal Trade Commission and the National Association of Attorneys

General joined forces in a nationwide effort to reduce telemarketing fraud. That joint effort included the establishment of an information clearinghouse so that government agencies could collect and share data about suspected telemarketing scams.

If you believe you have been the victim of a fraudulent telemarketing transaction, contact your local Better Business Bureau and the appropriate law enforcement authorities. Fast action is imperative – delays can allow the promoter to change name and locale, making apprehension, recovery, and prosecution even more difficult.

If the fraud is discovered in time, you may be able to stop payment on your check or contest charges on your credit card bill. If the scam involved the delivery of misrepresented merchandise, the recourses to office supply schemes outlined on pages 23 to 25 may prove effective. Recourses to phony invoice schemes and fraudulent charitable solicitations are outlined on pages 35 and 48. In the case of telemarketing investment fraud, seek advice and assistance from the state or federal agency that oversees activities in your area of concern – in commodity futures fraud, for example, contact the CFTC, your regional CFTC office, and the National Futures Association. If deceptive practices made use of the U.S. mail, also contact the Chief Postal Inspector, U.S. Postal Service. Addresses and phone numbers for these and other agencies and organizations can be found in Appendix A.

When fraud results in excessive, unauthorized charges on your company phone bill, as in PBX or 900-number scams, you may be able to work with your phone company or long-distance carrier to recoup losses. Many phone companies have a one-time policy of "forgiving" excessive charges from 900-number calls, and for large corporate customers, some long-distance carriers will go even farther to help absorb the cost of fraudulent calls.

Regardless of the nature of the fraud, you can help law enforcement officials combat telemarketing crime by sending a complete complaint, with details on the suspect company, to the offices of your state attorney general and local district attorney, listed in your phone directory, and to the Federal Trade Commission, Telemarketing Fraud Project, Room 200, 6th & Pennsylvania Avenue, N.W., Washington, D.C. 20580.

SECTION II

EXTERNAL
CRIME

CHAPTER 8

Product Counterfeiting

THE CASE OF
The Buyer's Blues

The buyer for a major chain of discount department stores knows that customers would snap up a hot-selling new line of blue jeans. The jeans, distributed under a well-known designer label, feature large gold-tone zippers on the pockets and sides of the legs and a sprightly devil patch on the back pocket. The problem is that the line's designer will only market her creations through certain selected retailers, and this discounter is not a part of that select list.

But the buyer has other sources – distributors who specialize in locating and purchasing hard-to-find products. Soon, in stores all around the country, customers find the discounter's racks filled with the popular designer jeans, selling at a price that is several dollars lower than that offered in most other area stores. Sales are brisk, and management and customers alike are pleased.

. . . Until the returns begin to come in. Customers begin bringing back their purchases for refunds, and their complaints are monotonously similar. After only one or two wearings, the jeans' stylish zippers loosen and fall off. The discounter is forced to refund so many of the defective garments that it finally yanks the product off store shelves. The distributor is contacted and proves uncommunicative and uncooperative. Appeals are made to the manufacturer, which sends a representative to examine the jeans. The examination confirms the manufacturer's suspicions; the blue jeans are counterfeits – very good counterfeits at first glance, with style and stitching copied to the last detail. A closer examination, however, reveals that the materials and workmanship are shoddy. The final tip-off is the back pocket patch. On the counterfeit jeans, the details on the devil's face and slippers are less defined. And he is carrying his pitchfork in the wrong hand.

An Epidemic of Fraud: From High Fashion to High Tech

The problem of commercial counterfeiting has reached epidemic proportions, according to the International Anticounterfeiting Coalition (IACC), a nonprofit organization consisting of over 120 U.S. and foreign manufacturing companies, legal and investigative firms, and trade associations. The International Trade Commission (ITC) estimates annual losses to U.S. businesses due to foreign counterfeiting and copyright and patent infringements at between $43 billion and $61 billion. That's an astounding 780 to 1,100 percent increase since 1982, when counterfeiters took in an estimated $5.5 billion, says the ITC.

The cost in U.S. jobs is just as alarming. In 1988, the U.S. Department of Commerce estimated that at least 750,000 jobs were lost nationwide as a result of product counterfeiting. Others suspect a much higher degree of damage. The "big three" automakers, for example, estimate that the counterfeiting of auto parts is responsible for the loss of about 240,000 jobs per year in the Detroit metropolitan area alone.

Whatever the figures, product counterfeiting clearly is a lucrative international business growing at an alarming rate, with devastating consequences for corporations and consumers in the U.S. and abroad.

Commercial counterfeiting began on a small scale with blue jeans, Swiss watches, and fashion accessories. Today, a wide range of products are involved, including cosmetics, sporting goods, tapes and CDs, drugs and medical equipment, aircraft parts, and Army missile systems parts.

The dangers go beyond the real economic hazards of lost domestic jobs and tax dollars. When a manufacturer's product is copied and mass-produced, the victimized company loses sales and profits. When a counterfeit product of inferior quality gives the consumer problems, the company suffers damage to perhaps its most priceless commodity – its reputation. And when the counterfeit is a shoddy copy of a heart pump, an automobile brake shoe, or a commercial helicopter or airliner part, health and safety are threatened.

Counterfeits and knockoffs are related sides of the same bad coin. Counterfeits are exact copies of a product, designed to have as great a similarity to the real thing – down to brand name and logotype – as the counterfeiter's art can achieve. Knockoffs are near-copies packaged to look just like the original, often including logo and emblems, but with a slight difference in the brand name or with the addition of the word "replaces" in extremely small type before the forged logo. The bogus goods may be imported as complete counterfeits, or labels, logos, and emblems may be applied after the items have entered the country.

Most production of counterfeits and knockoffs takes place in Far East countries, including Taiwan, Thailand, Indonesia, Singapore, Korea, Hong Kong, India, the Philippines, and the People's Republic of China. Other major sources include parts of Latin America (particularly Brazil, Colombia, and Mexico), the Middle East, and Africa. Industrialized nations make the list, too. For example, Italian counterfeiters provide more expensive, higher-quality look-alikes of luxury products targeted at middle- and high-income consumers. Thus product counterfeiting is very much an international phenomenon, with at least forty-four nations classed as producers, according to one U.S. survey.

In many ways, a company's success contributes to its vulnerability to the counterfeiting of its designs, trademarks, and copyrights. The counterfeiter's business is built on popular products with distinctive packaging and international recognition. Cashing in on the investment the manufacturer has made in research and development and in creating a demand in a particular market, the counterfeiter is able to mass-produce a copy at a cost far below that required to produce the real thing. Contributing to low costs are the illicit business's freedom from taxes, research and development expenses, advertising and promotional costs, and social security payments, plus its use of cheap labor, inferior materials, and shoddy construction.

While most copies are of inferior quality, in some cases the quality of a fake can be so good that even experts may have difficulty telling the difference. One area where counterfeiting is particularly hard to identify and prevent is in pirated computer software. Pirates can easily and inexpensively make copies of software that others have spent months or even years developing. Beyond the devastating losses in sales and profits, U.S. computer makers are concerned that the almost instantaneous theft and mass distribution of their creations could chip away at this country's position as a world leader in technology.

Cracking Down on Counterfeits

As long as there are cost-conscious consumers looking for brand names and distinctive designs at bargain prices – and unscrupulous companies and individuals ready to exploit that market – there will be counterfeiting. U.S. businesses and lawmakers hope only that efforts at prevention, detection, and retribution will increase the risks and lower the profits of the miscreants.

Many U.S. firms spend upwards of one million dollars annually to finance the war on counterfeiting. The most effective weapons in their arsenal include lawsuits against illicit overseas and domestic operations, detectives who gather and pass on leads, new anticounterfeiting technology, and consumer education.

Fighting counterfeiting through the differing legal systems of foreign countries requires a significant investment of time and money. While there has been some cooperation by a few of the developing nations considered primary sources of bogus goods, legislation and enforcement remain lax. Still, U.S. firms that have concertedly pursued suits against offenders in foreign countries have in some cases achieved a measure of success in stymieing the offenders. Private investigation firms have often played a vital role in providing the information needed to bring suit. Private detectives employed by U.S. and foreign firms monitor suspect factories and retail outfits and pass on leads that help the firms locate, close down, and sometimes prosecute the perpetrators.

New electronic, optical, and computer-designed technology also helps make the counterfeiter's job more difficult. Credit card companies employ laser technology that is expensive but effective (see Chapter 11, Credit Card Fraud). Recording companies are exploring the use of hard-to-imitate high-tech labels that contain thousands of microscopic lenses over a distinctive pattern or logo. One large automaker is experimenting with the use of holograms on its parts and packages. Other antifraud measures include "fingerprinted" labels, each printed with its own computer-generated code number; the authenticity of a label can be verified only by the system that generated its code number, thus enabling the manufacturer to easily identify counterfeits and the stores where they're being sold. Yet even with all these state-of-the-art devices, says the IACC, manufacturers are fighting an almost hopeless battle. As soon as a new technology is unveiled, counterfeiters begin to explore ways to imitate it – and most often, they succeed.

Intellectual Property Rights

An intellectual property right, as defined by the federal government, is the exclusive ownership of an original product of the thought processes. The four categories of intellectual property include:

- **Patents,** which are issued for a nonrenewable term of seventeen years (fourteen for design patents) to protect novel, useful, and nonobvious inventions. Examples range from a new type of kitchen gadget to a new process for manufacturing spaghetti to a new medicine or type of hybrid vegetable resulting from genetic engineering.

- **Trademarks,** which include designs, slogans, and brand names used to identify products or services as coming from a particular source. Once a trademark is in commercial use, it can be registered for a renewable term of ten years and thus is protected for as long as it remains in use.

- **Copyrights,** which protect original creations of authorship, such as books, music, original paintings, sound recordings, motion pictures, sculptures, and computer programs. In most cases, copyrights can be registered for a nonrenewable term consisting of the life of the author plus fifty years.

- **Mask works,** a new type of intellectual property that can be registered for a nonrenewable term of ten years. A mask work is the design of an electrical circuit, the pattern of which is transferred and fixed in a semiconductor chip during the manufacturing process.

In addition to these categories, federal law gives some recognition to **trade names,** which need not be registered. A trade name is a business name used by a manufacturer, merchant, or other party to identify its business or occupation. While trademarks and service marks identify the source of a product or service, trade names simply identify the producers themselves.

HOW TO PROTECT YOUR BUSINESS

The U.S. Customs Service helps businesses to protect their intellectual property, but it can only intervene if the property is registered with the proper federal agency. (Addresses for the federal agencies cited below can be found in Appendix A.)

- **Patents** are issued by the U.S. Patent and Trademark Office.

- **Trademarks** should be registered with the U.S. Patent and Trademark Office and recorded with the Customs Service.

- **Copyrights** should be registered with the U.S. Copyright Office and recorded with the Customs Service.

- **Mask works** should be registered with the Copyright Office; regulations are currently in preparation that will permit the recording of registered mask works with Customs.

- **Trade names** can be recorded with the Customs Service.

In addition to registering and recording your company's intellectual property, you can help foil product counterfeiters by following these measures:

1. Alert your sales force, distributors, and manufacturers to the counterfeiting problem, and instruct them to look for counterfeits at retail establishments and trade shows.

2. Educate consumers to the counterfeiting problem and how to distinguish the fakes. Investigate all consumer complaints about the inauthenticity of products.

3. Hire private investigators to monitor retail establishments for counterfeits and to find their sources. (See page 166 for tips on hiring an investigator.)

4. Encourage federal and state law enforcement and consumer agencies to aggressively pursue cases of product counterfeiting.

5. Set up a permanent department to investigate and prosecute counterfeiting cases.

For further advice, contact the IACC (see Appendix A), an organization involved in all aspects of intellectual property protection that provides members with information on investigation, counsel, litigation, detection techniques, and other key elements of an effective anticounterfeiting program.

The best approach retailers can take to avoid becoming a party to the distribution of bogus goods is founded on common sense. Deal with reputable distributors only, and be wary when a distributor says it will be easy delivering what you know is a hard-to-find product. If a deal seems too good to be true, it probably is.

WHAT TO DO IF YOU ARE VICTIMIZED

The most effective response to the counterfeiting of your company's designs, trademarks, and copyrights is multifaceted. Your actions should involve tracking down the source of the bogus goods, pushing for the enforcement of existing antifraud laws, and, through the measures discussed earlier, moving to prevent further counterfeiting.

Many manufacturers hire trademark and patent attorneys who use private detectives to locate the source of counterfeit products. The Customs Service also can assist patent owners in attempting to locate counterfeit importers by conducting a patent survey. For a fee ranging from $1,000 to $2,000, Customs will survey imports and provide the patent owner with the names and addresses of importers whose merchandise appears to infringe the patent. The information can be used in developing a patent infringement lawsuit and also in obtaining an ITC exclusion order.

If you are certain that one of your company's patents has been violated, you can apply to the ITC (see Appendix A) for an exclusion order, which directs the Customs Service to deny entry to imports in violation of the order. The ITC also can issue exclusion orders against goods imported by the use of other unfair trade practices, such as violation of trademark, copyright, and mask work registrations. Under recent revisions to the law, the ITC can direct that imports from repetitive violators be seized.

It is critical to consult your attorney in any case involving the investigation and prosecution of counterfeiting activities. The laws affecting intellectual property rights protection continue to evolve. Important federal legislation enacted in the past decade includes the Trademark Counterfeiting Act of 1984, which ensures criminal accountability for traffickers in counterfeit goods and services, counterfeit labels for phonorecords, and copies of motion pictures and other audiovideo works. This law allows for the charge of from $25,000 to $1,000,000 and up to five years' imprisonment for convicted product counterfeiters. Also, the 1984 Omnibus Trade and Competitiveness Act, together with a 1988 amendment, allows for trade retaliation against countries identified as refusing to protect intellectual property rights.

CHAPTER 9

Crimes Practiced on Cashiers

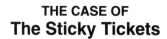

THE CASE OF
The Sticky Tickets

After a large weekend sale, the staff of a department store completes an inventory of remaining merchandise. A review of sales receipts and inventory sheets reveals that a large number of sale items that supposedly were sold remain on display, while similar nonsale items have disappeared.

After reviewing the situation with sales clerks and cashiers, the manager concludes that a number of dishonest customers must have peeled the price tags off sale items and transferred them to similar, but more expensive, nonsale items.

Cashiers, accustomed to looking at price tags rather than merchandise, rang up the more expensive items at the sale prices. As a result, inventory write-offs for this one major sale were more than $100,000.

Cashier Rip-offs:
A Retailer's Nightmare

Price tag switching is just one of the many ways businesses suffer at the hands of con artists and unscrupulous consumers. While the Department of Justice does not estimate dollar losses in crimes practiced on cashiers, its experience indicates that at some time virtually every business that transacts goods or services through a cashier or sales clerk will be victimized.

The list of crimes commonly practiced on cashiers and sales clerks includes:

- Quick-change scams
- Currency switches
- Counterfeit bill passing
- Price tag switches
- Container switches
- Refund and exchange fraud

HOW TO PROTECT YOUR BUSINESS

As is often the case in crimes practiced on retail businesses, the merchant's most effective recourse – indeed, sometimes the only recourse – is a staff aware of the methods of con artists and trained in recognizing and circumventing their schemes.

Quick-change Artists

The scheme. Quick change artists are criminals well versed in the art of fast-talking. Typically, the con artist will bring a small purchase to the cashier and offer to pay with a large denomination bill. As the cashier hands over the proper change, the con artist "discovers" that he has a smaller-denomination bill and withdraws the large bill. With his hands already on the change, he attempts, through a rapid exchange of money, to confuse the cashier into believing that the correct amount of money has changed hands. In reality, the con artist ends up walking away with all of the change from the small bill *plus* all or part of the change issued on the larger denomination.

Your defense. The best defense against a quick-change artist is an alert, cautious, "streetwise" cashier who understands the importance of taking time and not becoming rattled when money is being transacted.

The cash register should be well out of the reach of customers so a con artist cannot "assist" the cashier in making change. When the cashier rings up a sale, she should take the bill from the customer and place it on a safe but open spot away from the open cash drawer. The customer's money *should not be placed in the cash drawer.*

The cashier should count out the change at least twice, once to herself and a second time to the customer. If the customer attempts to exchange a small bill for the original large bill, the cashier should retrieve the change she was about to give the customer, return it to the cash register, and start over with the new bill. Until the sale has been completed, the customer's and cash register's money should not be mingled.

If the cashier becomes confused, she should close the cash drawer immediately and call for the store manager to assist in the transaction. Speed and confusion are the quick-change artist's allies – when complications develop, he will usually abandon the scam.

Currency Switches

The scheme. Currency switches are a form of counterfeiting, which is a federal offense. In most cases the con artist will attempt to pay for a purchase with a "raised note" – a bill that has been tampered with so that it appears to be of a higher denomination. For example, the con artist may hand over a bogus twenty-dollar bill that is actually a one-dollar bill. The illusion can be most convincing.

Typically, the con artist will take a number of twenty-dollar bills (or bills of another high denomination) and clip the numerical value from one corner of each bill. (The mutilated bills with three corners are still negotiable.) The clipped corners are then pasted over the corners of one-dollar bills and the edges sanded to blend color and texture. Some con artists apply the fake corners to only one side of the bill, hoping the cashier will not examine the other side.

Your defense. Cashiers should be alerted to the practice of currency switches and trained to examine bills quickly for counterfeits. A cursory examination of the look and feel of the corners of high-denomination bills, plus a glance to confirm that the correct face is pictured, should be sufficient to spot the impostors.

Counterfeit Bill Passing

The scheme. The counterfeiting of currency is one of the oldest crimes in history. In this century, however, modern photographic and printing devices have made the production of counterfeit money easier than ever.

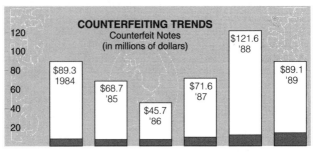

COUNTERFEITING TRENDS
Counterfeit Notes
(in millions of dollars)

- □ Seized Before Circulation
- ■ Passed on to the Public

Your defense. You can help to protect your business from the threat of counterfeit bill passing by becoming more familiar with United States currency. There are three types, or classes, of U.S. paper currency in circulation. The name of each class appears on the upper face of the bill. The different class bills are further identified by the color of their Treasury Seal and serial numbers.

COLOR OF TREASURY SEAL AND SERIAL NUMBER

CLASS		DENOMINATION
Federal Reserve Notes	**Green**	$1, $2, $5, $10, $20, $50, and $100
United States Notes	**Red**	$2, $5, and $100
Silver Certificates	**Blue**	$1, $5, and $10

Federal Reserve Notes account for 99 percent of all currency in circulation. United States Notes and Silver Certificates are no longer being printed.

Each denomination, regardless of class, has a prescribed portrait and back design, selected by the secretary of the treasury and the secretary's advisers:

$1	George Washington Great Seal of the United States	$20	Andrew Jackson White House
$2	Thomas Jefferson Declaration of Independence	$50	Ulysses S. Grant U.S. Capitol
$5	Abraham Lincoln Lincoln Memorial	$100	Benjamin Franklin Independence Hall
$10	Alexander Hamilton U.S. Treasury Building		

Notes of the $500, $1,000, $5,000 and $10,000 denomination have not been printed for many years and are being removed from circulation. The portraits appearing on these notes are McKinley on the $500, Cleveland on the $1,000, Madison on the $5,000, and Chase* on the $10,000.

Two new security features – a denominated security thread and microprinting – are being added to U.S. currency to help deter counterfeiting. The new features first appeared in $50 and $100 Federal Reserve Notes, Series 1990, and will be phased in gradually on all other denominations, with the possible exception of the $1 bill.

The **security thread** is embedded in the paper and runs vertically through the clear field to the left of the Federal Reserve seal on all notes except the $1 denomination. If it is decided to use the thread in the $1 denomination, it will be located between the Federal Reserve seal and the portrait.

On the $20 denomination and lower, the security thread reads "USA," followed by an identifier – e.g., "USA Twenty USA Twenty." Higher denominations have "USA" plus the numerical value – for example, "USA 50 USA 50" – repeated along the length of the thread. The thread and printing are easily seen when the bill is held up to a light source.

---

*Salmon Portland Chase (1808-73) was secretary of the treasury from 1861-64, during which period he created a national bank system.

NEW SECURITY FEATURES

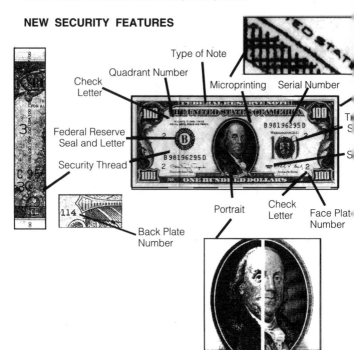

Type of Note

Quadrant Number

Check Letter

Microprinting   Serial Number

Federal Reserve Seal and Letter

Security Thread

Back Plate Number

Portrait

Check Letter

Face Plate Number

COUNTERFEIT	GENUINE
Portrait	
Appears lifeless, and background is usually too dark. Portrait merges into background. Hairlines not distinct. Additional solid line may be printed along sides of portrait.	Appears lifelike and stands out distinctly from fine, screenlike background. Hairlines are distinct. Under magnification, words "THE UNITED STATES OF AMERICA" appear along sides of portrait on $50 and $100 Federal Reserve Notes.
Federal Reserve and Treasury Seals	
Saw-toothed points on circumference are usually uneven, blunt, and broken off.	Saw-toothed points are even, clear, and sharp.

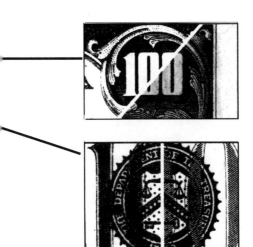

COUNTERFEIT	GENUINE
Serial Numbers	
May be in wrong color. May not be properly spaced or aligned.	Evenly spaced and aligned.
Border	
Fine lines that crisscross are not clear or distinct.	Fine lines are clear, distinct, and unbroken.
Paper	
Watermark may be seen. Red and blue lines may be printed on paper. When held to light, no security thread is seen.	No watermark. Red and blue fibers are imbedded in paper. Security thread appears when note is held to light.

Along with the addition of the security thread, a line of **microprinting** appears on the rim of the portrait on $50 and $100 denominations, beginning with Series 1990. The words "THE UNITED STATES OF AMERICA" are repeated along the sides of the portrait. As with the new security thread, the microprinting will be gradually phased in on all denominations, with the possible exception of the $1 bill. The microprinting can only be read with magnification; to the naked eye, it appears as little more than a solid line.

The best method of detecting a counterfeit bill is to compare the suspect note with a genuine bill of the same denomination and series, paying attention to the quality of printing and paper characteristics. *Look for differences, not similarities.*

Look for the **security thread** in the paper and for the **microprinting** by the portrait. Keep in mind, however, that it will be several years before these features appear on all currency.

Examine the tiny red and blue **fibers** imbedded in the paper of a genuine note. It is illegal to reproduce this distinctive paper. Often counterfeiters try to simulate these fibers by printing tiny red and blue lines on their paper. Close inspection reveals, however, that on the counterfeit the lines are printed on the surface, not imbedded in the paper.

Notice the **workmanship** of the note's design. Genuine money is made by the federal government's master craftsmen using expensive steel engraving and printing equipment designed for that purpose. Most counterfeiters use a photo mechanical or offset method to make a printing plate from a photograph of a genuine note. The resulting product looks flat and lacks fine detail.

Further, the lines in the portrait background, if you look closely, form squares. On counterfeits, some of these squares may be filled in, and many of the delicate lines in the portrait may be broken or missing.

Price Tag Switches

The scheme. In the early 1950's sticky-backed price tags came into widespread use and price tag switches joined the petty thief's bag of tricks. Con artists could discreetly peel off price tags and replace them with lower-priced tags while the merchandise was still on the shelf. The stamping of merchandise with prices in ink proved no more reliable an alternative. Con artists equipped with handkerchiefs soaked in ink remover could simply wipe the price off an item and give the cashier an inaccurate price. Another common ploy targeted primarily at grocery stores involves the switching of the ticketed lids of containers of similar products. For example, the plastic top of an expensive can of coffee can be switched with the top from a less expensive can before the item is brought to the cashier.

Your defense. The widespread use of UPC codes printed directly on product packages is the most effective deterrent to price tag switching. In stores where price tags still must be used, managers should ensure that the tags are affixed in a manner that makes them removable only by the cashier or only by being destroyed. On clothing, for example, garment tags affixed with plastic loops can be removed only by breaking the loop, and once the loop is broken the tag cannot be easily reattached. For prices placed directly on merchandise, sticky-backed labels are available that rip when removed and consequently cannot be reused.

Also effective, though expensive, is the use of electronic cash terminals hooked up with a central computer that contains current price information filed under stock numbers. Where cost makes the installation of these terminals impractical, it's a good idea to provide cashiers with current lists of sale items and prices. Cashiers should become familiar with these prices and should refer to the lists frequently.

Container Switches

The scheme. Container switches and price tag switches are closely related. In a container switch, the con artist removes the contents from a ticketed container and refills the container with a similar but higher-priced item. A shirt, for example, may be removed from its plastic bag and placed in a bag that originally contained a less expensive shirt.

In a variation of the container switch, the con artist opens a bag, box, or other container and conceals another item inside. A small, expensive toy, for example, may be hidden inside a box containing a less expensive toy, such as a model with numerous pieces. In grocery stores where customers bag their own produce, the container switch is a recurring and pervasive problem, with customers concealing expensive produce in bags of less costly items.

Your defense. Retail managers should make sure that product containers are tightly sealed and that when containers with broken seals are presented for purchase, they are opened and their contents examined. In grocery stores, cashiers should be made aware of the container switch and should be able to identify the different types of produce. Grocers should use transparent plastic bags for produce, and cashiers should be instructed to shake and check bags to be certain that other items have not been mixed in with less costly produce.

Refund and Exchange Fraud

The scheme. Refund and exchange fraud comes in many forms, including the following common schemes:

- Merchandise is shoplifted and then returned for a refund or exchange.
- A shoplifter collects discarded sales receipts, "lifts" items priced at the amounts shown on the salvaged receipts, and then returns the item, with receipts, for refund.
- An article is purchased by check; the customer stops payment on the check and before the check bounces, returns the article for a refund. (Also see Chapter 12, Check Fraud.)
- Merchandise that was broken or damaged by a customer is repackaged and returned for exchange, refund, or credit.
- An item purchased at one store is returned for credit to another store that sells the same item at a higher price.

Your defense. Some stores do not allow merchandise returns or exchanges, but most find that offering at least one or all of the three basic options – refund, exchange, and credit – is an important part of a good customer relations policy.

The BBB recommends that every business set a uniform returns policy based at least in part on the policies of the store's suppliers and on the local and state laws that govern refunds, exchanges, returns, warranties, and service contracts. Policies should be simple, understandable, and consistent and should be posted in a prominent location, such as over each cash register. Sales receipts, too, should carry a printed explanation of the store's policy. In some states and localities, consumer protection laws specify the acceptable manner of posting of merchants' refund and exchange policies.

Return policies should stipulate that, to return merchandise, the customer must have a cash register or credit card receipt as proof of purchase and that the merchandise must be in resalable condition, unless defects resulted from inferior product quality, not misuse by the customer.

On the return of high-priced items, many stores require that the refund be credited to the customer's charge account or that a refund check be sent to the customer's home address.

Exchange policies also should cover only merchandise that is in a condition to be resold or that contains defects for which the customer cannot be held responsible and should require at minimum a sales receipt, cash register receipt, canceled check, or other proof of purchase. There have been numerous cases of criminals purchasing bulk shipments of damaged or defective goods at a fraction of retail costs and returning the items for credit or exchanging them for nondefective products.

Returns for credit should require that merchandise be returned within a specified time period. Con artists have been known to purchase bulk quantities of out-of-date or out-of-style items at greatly reduced prices, only to return them for credit or refund.

WHAT TO DO IF YOU ARE VICTIMIZED

When the schemes described here are practiced on cashiers and are detected only after the fact, the merchant has little or no recourse. Even when a suspect is caught "in the act," there is little the merchant can do beyond preventing losses by short-circuiting the scheme.

In cases involving currency switches and counterfeiting, the cashier who is offered the bill should attempt to stall the suspect while the police or Secret Service are contacted. Note the suspect's description, the description of any companions, and the description and license number of any vehicle used. The cashier should initial and date the bill, and it should be placed in a protective cover and handed over to the police or Secret Service.

CHAPTER 10

Shoplifting

A CASE OF
Sticky Fingers

After taking a physical inventory, the owner of a bustling grocery store concludes that shoplifting is reducing his revenues by several hundred dollars each week. Aware that some area stores use convex mirrors placed in out-of-the-way spots to enable employees to keep an eye on potential shoplifters, the grocer decides to invest in several of these mirrors.

For several weeks after the mirrors are installed, shoplifting seems to subside. But within a few months, the incidence of pilferage reaches new heights. Determining that an even greater investment in his store's security is needed, the owner hires a uniformed security guard to walk the aisles. The impact is much the same – shoplifting subsides for a few weeks and then returns to previous levels.

Faced with the prospect of adding other, even more costly shoplifting deterrents, such as closed circuit television or plain-clothes security guards, the resigned store owner concludes that it will be more cost-effective simply to allow the problem to continue and write off shoplifting losses as a cost of doing business.

Shoplifter Profiles

Shoplifting jumped 35 percent in the four years from 1987 through 1990, according to FBI statistics, making it this country's fastest-growing larceny crime. Estimates of the cost to U.S. businesses vary dramatically, with figures ranging from $9 billion to $16 billion annually. All such estimates are at best educated guesses, however, since in the majority of cases, the crime of shoplifting goes undetected. In fact, according to one study, shoplifters are successful in getting away with the loot 97 percent of the time.

Shoplifting occurs primarily on the sales floors or at the checkout counters of retail stores. On the sales floor, nonprofessional shoplifters steal goods that can be quickly and easily hidden inside clothing, a backpack, or a pocketbook. Professional shoplifters – those for whom crime is a primary source of income – are much more skillful. Cleverly designed devices, such as clothing with large hidden pockets, "booster boxes" with a hinged side, and even shielded shopping bags for transporting merchandise with antitheft tags past detection gates, help the pro conceal items both small and large.

Most shoplifters are amateurs rather than professionals. **Juvenile offenders,** who, according to the Small Business Administration, account for about 50 percent of all shoplifting, may steal on a dare or simply for kicks. **Impulse shoplifters** include many "respectable" people who have not premeditated their thefts but instead succumb to the temptation of a sudden chance, such as an unattended dressing room or a blind aisle in a supermarket. **Alcoholics, vagrants, and drug addicts** are often clumsy and erratic in their behavior but may be violent as well – their apprehension is best left to the police. **Kleptomaniacs,** motivated by a compulsion to steal, usually have little or no actual use for the items they steal and in many cases could well afford to pay for them. All of these types of amateur shoplifters can be relatively easy to spot. The **professional shoplifter,** on the other hand, is usually highly skilled at the business of theft. Professionals generally steal items that can be resold quickly to an established fence, and they tend to concentrate on high-demand consumer goods such as televisions, stereos, and other small appliances. Even the professional, however, can be deterred from theft by a combination of alert personnel and effective store layout.

HOW TO PROTECT YOUR BUSINESS

For many years, businesses have used a number of protective devices and measures to try to detect and reduce shoplifting. Electronic sensing devices, closed circuit television, convex mirrors, uniformed and plain-clothes security guards, observation mirrors, and warning signs are among the more commonly used deterrents.

As part of a comprehensive, ever-changing program, these systems may prove effective in reducing the incidence of shoplifting. But, say many law enforcement authorities, there are more effective approaches. "Psychological deterrents" designed to make potential shoplifters feel uncomfortable and insecure about their actions may be more effective, and their overall cost is usually minimal when compared to the costs involved with mechanical or labor-intensive methods.

The following brief overview of various psychological and mechanical deterrents may help business owners determine which combination best suits their particular situation. We also urge you to contact your local police department for information on state laws concerning shoplifting and procedures to follow to prevent the crime.

Psychological Deterrents

☐ **Plan store layout with deterrence in mind.** Keep protruding "wings" and end displays low, not more than two or three feet high, and set display cases in broken sequences. Close and block off unused checkout aisles.

☐ **Cut down on the number of exits.** A store with many exits makes it easy for a shoplifter to slip out with merchandise. If compliance with local fire laws is a problem, exits may be converted to emergency exits. Attach noise alarms to unlocked exits.

☐ **Arrange the store so that everyone leaving must pass a checkout counter.** Check the lower racks of shopping carts, and, if possible, speak with customers as they leave. If a cashier suspects that someone is leaving the store with a concealed item, a question such as "May I help you with your purchase?" will unnerve a shoplifter without incriminating the employee if no shoplifting has occurred. (Also see Chapter 9, "Crimes Practiced on Cashiers.")

☐ **Keep displays neat by arranging products in rows rather than in disorganized piles.** When a display is organized, it is easier to spot when something is missing.

☐ **High-risk merchandise should be displayed behind counters, in locked cases, or on chained racks.** This includes electronic equipment, leather coats, and other items known to be particularly attractive to shoplifters. Customers should be shown only one valuable item at a time; a shoplifter can easily slip a small item into a sleeve or pocket.

☐ **Service-oriented establishments should instruct employees to greet customers as they enter the store** and to acknowledge waiting customers when busy with another customer. Shoplifters generally dislike being spoken to while they are "working," and personal attention often so unnerves them that they will leave without committing a crime.

☐ **Require customers to "check" packages and other containers while shopping.** In grocery stores, prevent concealment of stolen items beneath produce by using clear plastic bags.

☐ **Be alert in distracting situations.** Juvenile and professional shoplifters often work in groups. One shoplifter will create a disturbance, such as an "accident" or argument, and while employees are distracted, the other will make off with the goods.

☐ **Train your employees to be alert to these warning signals:**

• Customers with bulky packages, shopping bags, large boxes, oversized arm slings, or other possible concealment devices.

• Shoppers walking with short or unnatural steps, who may be concealing items between their legs.

- Groups of shoppers who enter a store together, then break up and go separate ways, or customers who attempt to monopolize a salesperson's attention.

- Customers who handle a lot of merchandise without reaching a decision, linger in one area, wander aimlessly through the store, or consistently shop during hours when store staff is lighter than usual.

☐ **Consider an employee training program.** A watchful salesperson can be your most effective antitheft tool. Local law enforcement officials may be able to help you to set up a program for training employees in identifying potential shoplifters, approaching them without unlawfully accusing them, and, if necessary, preventing them from leaving with stolen goods. The emphasis in a training program should be on preventing the crime rather than on surveillance with the intent of apprehending the criminal. In any case, employees should not be asked to apprehend shoplifting suspects.

Protective Devices and Systems

☐ **Signs that warn against shoplifting** have mixed results. In some instances, these signs, which usually contain a description of state laws against shoplifting, may help to scare off some young offenders. But more experienced offenders seem to ignore the signs, and some reports indicate that the incidence of shoplifting actually increases after signs are put in place.

☐ **Convex mirrors** that expose hard-to-see corners of the store have limited success as deterrents. While the mirrors allow employees to keep an eye on suspected shoplifters, they also allow shoplifters to watch employees – and when the employee isn't looking, the crime is committed.

☐ **Uniformed guards** often prove effective at first, but once professional shoplifters have had time to observe and adapt to the guards' habits, the deterrence factor diminishes. Stationary guards posted at all exits are most effective.

☐ **Plain-clothes guards** seem to be more effective than uniformed guards in the apprehension of shoplifters. They have the advantage of being able to stay close to suspected offenders; once professional shoplifters ascertain their identity, however, plain-clothes guards lose this advantage.

☐ **One-way mirrors** can be installed in balcony office areas, enabling the office to be used as an observation post by management or security personnel. Some large retailers install one-way mirrors on large, hollow columns and place security personnel inside. These systems are expensive to operate on a full-time basis but have proven effective in identifying shoplifters.

☐ **Peepholes** also are costly to operate, but they may be used effectively in specific problem areas.

☐ **Closed circuit television cameras** often have proven effective in deterring nonprofessional offenders, but some law enforcement authorities caution that professionals may react to them in the same way they do to uniformed guards – by learning how to commit the offense out of view. Some retailers combat that problem by hiding cameras inside smoked-glass ceiling domes or in other hard-to-spot locations. One new system even plants closed circuit cameras inside mannequins. Some stores hold down costs by installing impressive-looking, effective deterrent systems that use both genuine cameras and "dummies."

☐ **Electronic sensing devices** are among the most effective of the deterrent systems. The reusable heavy white plastic antitheft tags are stapled onto merchandise in a manner that makes them difficult to remove. Other "invisible" tags must be deactivated by being passed over a device at the checkout counter. Some of these systems work like airport metal detectors – the tag contains metal or another material that, when passed through a pair of pedestals broadcasting radio signals, reflects the signal and sets off an alarm. While an effective deterrent, the tag system has its drawbacks. Tags are expensive, and they are time-consuming to attach and remove. A determined thief usually can remove them with a pair of pliers or other easily concealed equipment. Also, false alarms can embarrass honest customers and sometimes lead to unlawful-arrest suits. Some retailers address the latter problem by positioning trained employees near detection gates during high-traffic periods. Others are using a new system that replaces the familiar plastic

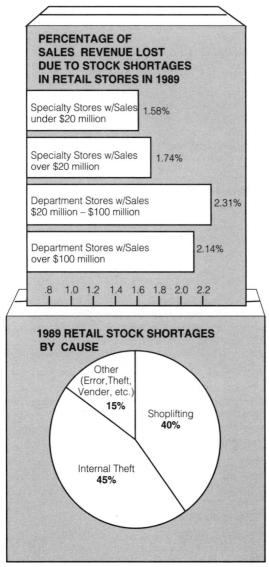

PERCENTAGE OF
SALES REVENUE LOST
DUE TO STOCK SHORTAGES
IN RETAIL STORES IN 1989

Specialty Stores w/Sales under $20 million — 1.58%

Specialty Stores w/Sales over $20 million — 1.74%

Department Stores w/Sales $20 million – $100 million — 2.31%

Department Stores w/Sales over $100 million — 2.14%

.8 1.0 1.2 1.4 1.6 1.8 2.0 2.2

1989 RETAIL STOCK SHORTAGES BY CAUSE

Other (Error, Theft, Vender, etc.) **15%**

Shoplifting **40%**

Internal Theft **45%**

Source: National Retail Federation

antitheft tags with an updated version containing a lithium-battery-powered computer chip. When the tag is tampered with or passed through a detection gate, it sends a message to the security department and begins to beep, enabling security to pick out the one shoplifter among a crowd of innocent shoppers. Other new electronic antitheft devices include a tag the size of a strand of hair that can be hidden on a bar code or price sticker and a plastic "ink tag" containing vials of indelible ink – when the tag is removed improperly, the vials burst, leaving a stain on both the merchandise and the would-be thief.

WHAT TO DO IF YOU ARE VICTIMIZED

Laws against shoplifting differ in each of the fifty states and are continually changing. We recommend that you contact your state or local police department for up-to-date information on the laws of your own state. Also follow these basic guidelines from the Small Business Administration:

1. Remember that, for shoplifting charges to have a chance of prevailing, you must be able to see the suspect take or conceal merchandise, identify the merchandise as yours, testify that it was taken with the intention to steal, and prove that it was not paid for. Otherwise, you may leave yourself open to countercharges of false arrest.

2. Also keep in mind that false arrest need not mean police arrest. Simply preventing a person from conducting normal activities can be deemed false arrest. Further, any physical contact – even a light touch on the arm – may be considered unnecessary and used against you in court.

3. In general, store personnel should never accuse customers of stealing nor should they try to apprehend suspected shoplifters. If they observe suspicious behavior or an apparent theft in progress, they should alert the store owner, manager, security personnel, or the police.

4. It is wisest to apprehend shoplifters outside the store. You will have a better case if you can show that the shoplifter left the store with stolen merchandise. Outside apprehension also eliminates unpleasant scenes that might disrupt normal store operation. However, you may prefer to apprehend a shoplifter inside the store if the merchandise involved is of considerable value or if you feel that the thief may be able to elude you outside the store premises.

5. Do not accuse the suspect of shoplifting. Rather, identify yourself, and say, "I believe you have some merchandise that you have forgotten to pay for. Would you mind coming with me to straighten things out?"

6. When cornered, the first thing most shoplifters – amateur or pro – will say is "I've never done this before." In general, this should give you more reason, if your evidence is sufficient, to call the police and proceed with prosecution. Failure to prosecute first offenders may encourage them to try again. In addition, rumors may spread that your store is an "easy hit."

7. Some organizations have control files on shoplifters who have been caught. You can check these files to see whether the person you catch has a prior record. Your retail merchants' association can inform you about the services available in your area.

8. Naturally, each situation must be handled differently and your good judgment is required. You may wish to release a shoplifter when there's some indication that the person could honestly have forgotten to pay for the merchandise. Prosecution may be necessary, however, if the shoplifter is violent, if he or she lacks proper identification and you suspect a prior record, if he or she appears to be under the influence of alcohol or drugs, if the theft involves merchandise of great value, or if the shoplifter appears to be a professional.

9. Juvenile shoplifters require special handling. A strict, no-nonsense demeanor often makes a lasting impression on the young offender and may deter future theft.

Sharing the Costs of Deterrence

By the end of 1990, thirty-nine states had adopted laws allowing retailers to send **civil demand letters** to accused shoplifters, and several other states were considering similar antishoplifting statutes. A civil demand letter pledges that a retailer will refrain from suing for civil damages if the accused returns the stolen merchandise and pays a penalty of $100 to $200. According to one security expert, the statute has been a significant deterrent to juvenile theft.

CHAPTER 11

Credit Card Fraud

THE CASE OF
The Card Crook

A restaurant owner in need of operating capital answers an ad in the business section of his newspaper promising a substantial commission for credit card processing. He soon finds himself meeting with a well-dressed and personable businessman who explains that, because of the unsavory reputation of some telemarketers, he has been unable to establish a credit card merchant account for his new business, which involves telephone sales of vitamins and water purifier systems. If he can't accept credit card orders, he can't do business. He is willing, therefore, to pay the restaurant owner a handsome fee each month for simply allowing him to process his customers' credit card orders through the restaurant's account.

It sounds like a good deal. And for several weeks, all goes well. The restaurant owner processes the telemarketer's bank drafts, passes along payments, and receives his first one thousand dollars in commissions. Then he finds himself hit with a flood of chargebacks. Repeated calls to the telemarketer's business number go unanswered, and when he tracks down the address he was given, he finds an abandoned back office. The chargebacks resulting from the complaints of customers who received worthless merchandise from the telemarketer continue to roll in. To make matters worse, the restaurant owner is contacted by his bank to explain the marked increase in his business.

Confessing to the credit laundering arrangement, the beleaguered restaurateur finds his merchant account terminated. The action turns out to be unnecessary – facing thousands of dollars in chargebacks, the owner ends up losing not only his credit and his reputation but his business as well.

The Credit Card Revolution

According to the National Association of Credit Card Merchants, the purchasing power, or combined credit limits, of all credit cards in the United States equals three times the value of all currency in circulation. This purchasing power is spread out over one billion credit cards, with 140 million Americans holding at least one card and most having several.

According to the Federal Trade Commission (FTC), the cost of credit and charge card fraud to cardholders and card companies may be as high as $500 million a year. Credit card fraud losses for MasterCard alone increased to $300 million in 1990, nearly doubling 1989 losses and reflecting a 15 percent increase in card fraud activity. Sixty percent of that fraud took place in retail stores, clothing stores, and miscellaneous retail sales.

Banks, department stores, and oil companies that issue credit cards all feel the brunt of these financial losses. The American Bankers Association estimates that the average loss per bank in 1989 ranged from $2,000 for banks with under $3 million in assets to an estimated $280,000 for banks with assets over $1 billion. Affected businesses include not only the

CREDIT SALES ARE UP FOR DEPARTMENT STORES......................

	1985	1986	1987	1988	1989
Cash	9.2%	12.2%	10%	14.2%	11.9%
Third party credit	38.9%	36.6%	40%	41.%	38.5%
Credit	51.8%	51.2%	50.0%	44.8%	49.0%

Source: National Retail Federation

CREDIT SALES ARE DOWN FOR SPECIALTY STORES ....

	1985	1986	1987	1988	1989
Cash	17.3%	22.7%	17.0%	12.3%	14.7%
Third party credit	46.9%	48.6%	51.0%	40.9%	56.2%
Credit	35.8%	28.7%	32.0%	46.8%	29.1%

Source: National Retail Federation

nation's retailers, but also restaurants, hotels, airlines, travel agents, car rental companies, mail-order companies, and other businesses that cannot survive without accepting credit cards.

It is the consumer who ultimately picks up the tab when credit fraud losses are passed along in the form of higher prices. Further, consumers generally are liable for up to $50 of unauthorized charges per card if their cards are lost or stolen and the credit card issuer is not notified before the charges are made.

Profiles of Credit Card Fraud

Perpetrators of credit card fraud – the illegal use of stolen or counterfeit credit cards – fit no one mold. From seemingly honest merchants to underworld figures, they each have their own peculiar method of operation. The con artist commonly will use the stolen or counterfeit card for only a few days and then discard it, but even that practice varies. Following are profiles of several "typical" credit card criminals.

Credit Card Laundering

> **BUSINESS OWNERS: My company needs MasterCard, Visa and Am Ex processing. $1,000 per week guaranteed commission. Call L.F. at 555-2230.**

Would you extend an unlimited, unsecured line of credit to another business that could not get credit from a bank? If you decide to answer an ad like this and agree to deposit another company's credit card sales drafts into your merchant account, that is what you have done. You are taking a financial risk that a bank was unwilling to take.

Credit card laundering, also called draft laundering or factoring, works like this: A company – often a telemarketer – that cannot obtain a credit card merchant account recruits another company to process its credit card transactions through its own merchant account. When the processing merchant receives payment for the credit card charges, it turns over the payment to the company without an account, retaining an agreed-upon percentage or other fee.

This seemingly simple procedure for earning extra cash can have disastrous consequences for the draft processing merchant. The risks include:

● **Financial loss.** When you agree to process other merchants' credit card charges, you take on the responsibility of paying for any chargebacks. Financial losses can be huge, sometimes even forcing victimized merchants out of business.

● **Credit loss.** Depositing third-party sales drafts is a violation of your merchant agreement. Even if there are no customer complaints or chargebacks, you risk losing your credit card merchant account if the arrangement is discovered.

● **Legal risk.** If the company whose credit card drafts you agree to launder engages in fraudulent activities, you could find yourself facing criminal prosecution.

If you are approached by a business proposing a draft laundering arrangement, you can protect your business and help rid the marketplace of fraud by reporting the contact to your bank or credit card company.

A youth spends several weeks traveling across the country, living off purchases made on credit cards found in a wallet stolen from the front seat of a car.

The operators of a credit fraud ring steal legitimate but blank credit cards and imprint them with the names and numbers of active accounts, obtained from operatives at a credit bureau. The counterfeit cards are used by thieves and other criminals to buy airline tickets or pay for hotel rooms as they travel to commit crimes nationwide.

A hustler makes his living using inexpensive equipment to erase the data from the magnetic stripes on stolen credit cards and reencode illegally obtained information from valid cards onto the stolen ones.

A team of underworld loan sharks acquires legitimate businesses and pushes them into insolvency; a key part of their scheme involves running the companies' credit cards to their spending limits before filing for bankruptcy. (See chapter 5 for further details on bankruptcy fraud.)

A merchant uses an electronic point-of-sale terminal to manually key in fraudulent credit card charges, defrauding banks of over one million dollars.

An individual searches through a restaurant's trash for carbons from used credit card forms and uses the numbers to charge merchandise over the phone or by mail.

 ## HOW TO PROTECT YOUR BUSINESS

Credit card issuers are fighting fraud with concerted prevention and detection efforts. One of the most significant improvements in the past few years was the introduction of bankcards with the hologram. Counterfeiters have found this feature too difficult to duplicate and, as a result, the number of illegally reproduced cards has declined dramatically.

Today, however, new forms of counterfeiting continue to threaten the credit card industry. These include magnetic stripe counterfeiting, altered signature panels, and reembossed account numbers. Magnetic stripe counterfeiting is one of the most serious problems. In this form of fraud, the data from a stolen card's magnetic stripe is erased and replaced with illegally obtained information from a valid card. In most cases, it is impossible for a cashier to detect that the magnetic stripe has been altered.

The process is endless: As bankcard issuers come up with new security features, counterfeiters come up with increasingly sophisticated methods for defeating card security. Special features being introduced by one major card issuer to combat the proliferation of altered cards include:

☐ A mandatory **tamper-evident signature panel,** to be incorporated in all newly issued cards beginning in mid-1992. The panel will discolor immediately if any attempt is made to tamper with the signature or indent printing on it.

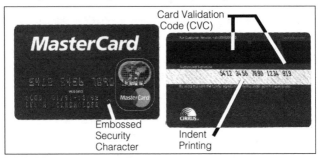

Card Validation Code (CVC)

Embossed Security Character

Indent Printing

☐ An optional **Enhanced Card Security Package,** which banks can incorporate in the cards they issue. The package includes:

• An **embossed security character,** to alert sales clerks – and would-be counterfeiters – that the card has the new package of security enhancements.

• **Indent printing** on the signature panel, in a unique reversed italic font that makes alteration extremely difficult. The indent printing matches the embossed account information on the front of the card.

• Two **Card Validation Codes** (CVCs), one encoded onto the magnetic stripe and one indent-printed on the signature panel. The CVCs enable the card issuer and the sales clerk using a point-of-sale computer terminal to immediately recognize a counterfeit card.

In addition to new security features, card issuers offer a variety of security programs designed to help businesses detect and forestall fraudulent transactions.

Many of these security programs require the use of electronic point-of-sale (POS) verification systems. About 80 percent of all credit card transactions today are processed electronically. High-tech electronic systems allow retailers to verify credit card numbers without a phone call to credit card centers for authorization. Many of the systems use a POS terminal that "reads" the magnetic stripe on a credit card and automatically telephones a system computer; within a few seconds, the terminal receives validation or rejection of the card. In many cases, transaction information also is transferred to the merchant's bank immediately or at the end of the business day.

To protect your business from credit card fraud, familiarize yourself with the fraud prevention programs available from your credit card issuer. Electronic point-of-sale systems provide the most effective protection against fraud. If you do not use electronic authorization, the following steps can help you combat credit card fraud:

1. Examine all credit cards presented, verifying that the expiration date has not been reached and the customer's signature matches the signature on the card.

2. Check all account numbers in the card recovery bulletins provided by card issuers.

3. Check carbon copies to make certain imprints are clear.

4. Establish a floor limit beyond which transactions require telephone authorization.

5. Be wary of customers who make numerous small purchases just under the floor limit; random authorization checks on small purchases may help detect fraud.

WHAT TO DO IF YOU ARE VICTIMIZED

Credit cards are the property of their issuing companies. Those who legally carry and use credit cards do so with the permission and authorization of the issuer. Therefore, a credit card company will instruct a merchant who is presented with a card that is being used in an unauthorized manner to refuse to allow the purchase and often will further authorize the merchant to confiscate the card. Most issuing institutions emphasize the importance of the merchant's attempt to retain the card and thus prevent its further illegal use, but they also caution that an effort should be made to confiscate a card only if it seems reasonably safe to do so. If not, the merchant should try to discreetly copy the card's account and Bank Identification Numbers and any other pertinent information (the suspect's name, address, driver's license number, etc.) before returning the card.

Some credit card companies have a special system for merchants to use when fraud is suspected. For example, the cashier may call the card issuer's voice authorization center, using a fraud-alert code number to identify the authorization request, and receive instructions on how to proceed. In the absence of instructions from the credit card issuer, a merchant should attempt to stall an individual using a stolen or counterfeit card for as long as possible without resorting to physical detention. While the suspect is "waiting for verification of the card," the merchant or cashier should inconspicuously telephone the police. If the suspect insists on leaving before the police arrive, the merchant should try to get a license number and description of the car or other vehicle used. A detailed description of the suspect and any companions and an indication of the direction taken by car or on foot also will be helpful to the police.

A merchant who correctly processes a bankcard transaction is relieved of further financial liability. Should a problem develop with the transaction – for example, the customer has exceeded the card's credit limit – the card issuer absorbs the risk. However, merchants who suffer losses by not following stipulated verification procedures may have difficulty recovering lost funds. Some credit card issuers may agree to reimburse some initial losses, but businesses that frequently bypass the transaction verification procedure may be forced to cover their own losses.

CHAPTER 12

Check Fraud

 ### THE CASE OF
The Friendly Forger

A well-dressed woman visits a gift shop and seeks out the store manager. She is visiting family in the area, is shopping for gifts, and has run out of cash. It is Saturday and the banks are closed, so she is hoping the merchant will allow her to pay for her purchase with an out-of-state check, made out for fifty dollars over the purchase price so she can buy a few items elsewhere.

The manager is sympathetic. If she can provide some identification, he will be glad to help her. The woman presents several credit cards, from which he carefully copies the numbers. As an added precaution, he asks for the local address of the woman's relatives. The purchase is made and the check cashed.

On Monday the check is deposited; on Wednesday the manager receives a call from his bank. The check is no good – the signature has been forged and, it turns out, the check comes from a checkbook stolen a week earlier along with several credit cards and various personal possessions.

The merchant is forced to absorb the lost fifty dollars cash and twenty-five-dollar purchase. The woman's "local address" does not exist, and she is never found.

Types of Bad Checks

Schemes involving the passing of bad checks have always figured among the most prevalent forms of crime against banks and business. With check writing on the rise – estimates put the total number of checks written in 1989 at nearly fifty-one billion and project that figure may top fifty-seven billion in 1992 – the opportunity for fraud continues to grow. An estimated five hundred million forged checks are negotiated annually, according to the U.S. Department of Justice, and in 1989 and 1990, the passing of bad checks cost financial institutions and retail establishments approximately $10 billion.

Virtually any type of check, whether written for the payment of a bill, a federal or state tax refund, a payroll, welfare benefits, or the purchase of goods or services, can be fraudulently redeemed. The five most common types of bad checks are:

1. **Checks drawn on insufficient funds.** An individual or business issues a check – intentionally or unknowingly – on a bank account without the funds to cover it.

2. **Checks drawn on closed accounts or no account.** These are often evidence of fraud, although in some cases they may be the result of extreme carelessness on the part of the customer.

3. **Completely falsified checks.** The person passing the check may have fabricated or printed it and usually forges the signatures and endorsements. These checks often are drawn on nonexistent bank accounts – sometimes even the bank itself does not exist.

4. **Legitimate checks that have been falsified.** Legitimate checks, already filled out and signed, are stolen from homes, offices, or the mail and are then altered or forged. The amount of the legitimate check can be increased by altering a figure or adding a zero.

5. **Checks falsified on legitimate bank accounts.** These include stolen blank checks and high-quality photocopies or other reproductions of legitimate blank checks. The swindler fills out the check, forging the signature of the account holder.

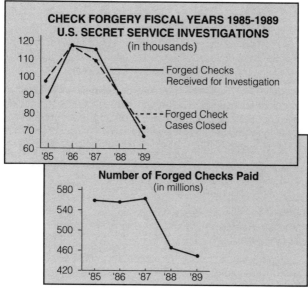

Source: United States Secret Service

Variations of Check Fraud

The following are only a few examples of the many variations of check fraud:

☐ A dishonest employee or other individual gains access to a company's check writing machine and executive signature imprinter. This equipment is used to make up seemingly legitimate checks on the company's account, with checks often taken from the back of the checkbook so their absence will not be noticed.

☐ A bad check – either completely falsified or drawn on a legitimate account with insufficient funds – is sent as payment for a mail-order purchase. By the time the check "bounces," the order has been received and the recipient has vanished.

☐ The recipient of a check increases its face value by altering or adding to existing numbers and wording.

☐ Con artists create a phony company that pays other legitimate businesses with fraudulent checks drawn on insufficient funds or nonexistent bank accounts. Many businesses will provide goods or services and accept checks as payment from another business, even one previously unknown, without verifying that the company actually exists.

☐ A "customer" presents a stolen or fraudulent check at a check cashing window or grocery store. Often these checks are "paid" toward a purchase, inducing the merchant to cash the check in order to make the sale.

☐ A neatly dressed stranger pays for a pair of shoes with a U.S. Government check. He then moves on to other stores and cashes several more government checks – all stolen from individual mailboxes.

☐ Bogus payroll checks are cashed on payday at the bank at which the company that supposedly issued them maintains its payroll account.

☐ Stolen traveler's checks are redeemed, usually with no identification required.

HOW TO PROTECT YOUR BUSINESS

Businesses that establish, maintain, and advertise firm check cashing policies generally have few problems with bad checks. The following precautions make effective guidelines in a policy aimed at combatting check fraud:

1. **Set guidelines regarding the types of checks your business will accept.** Businesses are likely to receive eight different kinds of checks:

   • A **personal check** is written and signed by the individual offering it; the check should be made out to your firm.

   • A **two-party check** is issued by one party – the maker – to a second party who endorses it so that it may be cashed by a third party. This type of check is susceptible to fraud because, among other reasons, the maker can stop payment at the bank.

- A **payroll check** usually is imprinted with the name of the employer and a number. In most cases, the word "payroll" is also printed on the check. The employee's name is printed by a check writing machine or typed. Except in the case of a small community where you know the company officials and employee personally, you should not cash a payroll check that is hand printed, rubber-stamped, or typewritten.

- A **government check** is issued by the federal, state, or local government to cover salaries, tax refunds, pensions, welfare allotments, veterans' benefits, etc. Because of the prevalence of stolen and forged government checks, some banks refuse to cash Social Security, welfare, relief, or income tax checks unless the customer has an account with the bank. Losses from government check theft and forgery amount to millions of dollars annually. Always insist on proper identification when U.S. Government checks are cashed, examine the identification closely, and be aware that all U.S. Government checks issued on or before October 1, 1989 are void after one year and should no longer be cashed.

- A **blank check,** also known as a **universal check,** is no longer acceptable to most banks, due to Federal Reserve Board regulations that prohibit standard processing without the encoded characters. Universal checks require a special collection process by the bank.

- A **counter check** is issued by a few banks to depositors when they withdraw funds from their accounts. Some stores have their own counter checks for the convenience of customers. Counter checks are not negotiable and should be so marked.

- A **traveler's check** is sold with a preprinted amount to travelers who do not want to carry large amounts of cash. The traveler signs the checks at the time of purchase and should countersign them only in the presence of the person who cashes them. Do not accept traveler's checks that have been endorsed in advance. Require another signature while you watch. Also remember that all "traveler's checks" are not necessarily legitimate. Check fraud artists know that many merchants believe that even stolen traveler's checks will be redeemed by the issuing company. In fact, in most cases, the major traveler's check companies will honor stolen traveler's checks that have been accepted unknowingly by a merchant. However, if the endorsement of the stolen check does not closely resemble the authorized signature, the check issuer may refuse to redeem the check. If in doubt, merchants can refuse to accept traveler's checks or can request valid photo identification and record identification data on the check. Finally, be wary of situations in which many traveler's checks are cashed at one time.

- A **certified check** carries on its face the bank's guarantee of the validity of the signature and the availability of the funds. Certified checks can be forged, however, and you should not hesitate to contact the bank for verification. If you cannot contact the bank and you have serious doubts about the check's authenticity, refuse to accept it. With a certified personal or business check, insist on identification with a photo and signature.

In addition, **money orders** may be passed as checks. However, money orders usually are sent in the mail, and most stores do not accept them in face-to-face transactions. Some small stores sell money orders. If yours does, never accept a personal check in payment.

2. **Examine the check carefully**. The extra effort involved in carefully scrutinizing every check can pay off. When a personal check is presented to you directly, insist that it be written and signed in front of you. Don't be misled into assuming that a check made out with a check writing machine or typewriter is legitimate. Look for these key items on every check:

- **Location.** Look first to make certain the check shows the name, branch, town, and state where the bank is located. Use extra care in examining a check that is drawn on a nonlocal bank; require positive identification, and list the customer's local and out-of-state addresses and phone numbers on the back of the check.

- **Date.** Examine the date for accuracy, and do not accept checks that are undated, postdated, or more than thirty days old.

- **Amount.** Make sure the numerical amount agrees with the written amount. Personal checks should be for the exact amount of the purchase – the customer should receive no change. Set a limit on the amount you will accept on a check, based on the amount of your average sale, and make it a policy that any check over the limit must be approved by management. Be aware, however, that most bad-check passers pass checks for twenty-five to thirty-five dollars, on the assumption that retailers are more cautious when accepting large checks.

- **Legibility.** Checks should be written and signed in ink and should not have any erasures or written-over amounts. Do not accept checks that are not written legibly.

- **Types of merchandise.** Be watchful of the types of merchandise purchased. When a customer makes random selections of merchandise or shows no concern about prices, be doubly cautious when a check is offered for payment.

- **Low-sequence numbers.** Experience indicates that a higher number of low-sequence checks are returned. Most banks that issue personalized checks begin the numbering system with 101.

3. **Always insist on proper identification.** Some stores demand at least two pieces of identification. It is important to get enough identification so the person presenting the check can be identified and located if it turns out to be worthless. However, keep in mind, if a check is stolen or forged, the identification presented may be, too. The following can be useful forms of identification:

- **Driver's license.** If licenses in your state do not carry photographs, you may want to ask for a second ID.

- **Auto registration card.** Make sure the state name is the same for the registration card and the bank.

- **Credit cards or shopping plates.** These can be used as identification if they bear a signature or laminated photograph. The customer's credit card number should not be written on the back of the check, however. That common practice creates an opportunity for credit fraud, since thieves who gain access to the check as it travels through the clearing process acquire all the information needed to charge merchandise to the consumer or apply for credit in the consumer's name. Credit card data noted on checks rarely helps the retailer locate a bad-check passer, anyway, since most banks will not provide merchants with information on cardholders. Further, the major credit card companies strictly forbid merchants from charging a purchase to a customer's credit card when a check bounces.

- **Government passes.** Picture identification cards should carry the name of the employing department and a serial number. Building passes should carry a signature as well.

- **Identification cards.** Cards issued by the armed services, police departments, schools, and companies should carry a photo, description, and signature. Police cards also carry a badge number.

The following forms of ID either were never intended for identification or are easily forged and thus should not be accepted: Social Security cards, business cards, insurance cards, birth certificates, library cards, voter registration cards, learner's permits for driving.

Some large stores photograph each person who cashes a check, along with the person's identification. Some also verify addresses and phone numbers in the local phone directory or with the information operator when in doubt about a check.

4. **Compare signatures.** Regardless of the type of identification you require, it is essential that you compare the signature on the check with that on the identification. You also should compare the person standing before you with any photograph and/or description on the ID. Do not accept checks that have been signed with a rubber stamp unless you are familiar with the person presenting the check – even then it is a good idea to have the check signed again in front of you. When examining signatures, by wary of:

- Signatures that appear out of character for the individual cashing the check, such as a small, precise signature from a young boy or large man. When in doubt, ask the person to sign again in front of you, and watch how he or she signs.

- Individuals who take extreme care and much time signing their names.

- Customers who try to distract you while they are signing the check or while you are examining it.

5. **Set a policy for cashing checks and review these procedures with employees frequently.** Your policy might include:

   - **Requiring management's approval** before salespeople can cash checks.

   - **Using a rubber stamp,** like the one below. Many retailers require that the back of all checks be stamped and the appropriate information filled in.

Print			
Salesperson-Name and No.			
Auth. Signature			
Customer's Address			
Home Phone		Business Phone	
Ident. No. 1			
Ident. No. 2			
Dept No.		Amount of Sale	
Take	Send	COD	Will Call

   - **Verifying checks through the issuing bank.** Some banks will perform this service only for depositors.

   - **Verifying checks through a check verification service.** In the past few years, thousands of small U.S. businesses have installed electronic check verification systems. These new, high-tech systems allow cashiers to validate checks and credit cards at the register, usually in just a few seconds. The systems use a variety of technologies, including computer networks and satellite linkups. Some compare account numbers with a computer-stored list of customers who have been approved for check cashing privileges; others access national lists of bad-check passers. Some verification services even offer a money-back guarantee on any bad check approved by the system. Before contracting with a check verification service, ask the service to provide proof from the Federal Trade Commission that it complies with the Fair Credit Reporting Act.

6. **Consider the use of check cashing cards,** which may be offered to customers after an initial credit check with local banks and credit checking agencies.

7. **Safeguard your business and personal checkbooks and check writing equipment.** Store bank statements and canceled checks in a secure location, and periodically look at the back of your company's checkbook to make certain no checks are missing.

8. **Never discriminate when refusing a check.** Don't tell a customer that you cannot accept a check because, for example, he or she is a college student or lives in a bad neighborhood. If you do, you may be in violation of state or federal laws against discrimination.

WHAT TO DO IF YOU ARE VICTIMIZED

As in most white-collar crimes, the likelihood that a business will recoup money lost in a check fraud scheme depends on the actions taken as soon as the scheme is detected. Precaution is always your best defense – and in the case of check fraud, it often is your only defense. Even given state and federal laws, once a bad check has been passed, it is at best very difficult to recoup lost revenues.

Insufficient Funds

Most checks returned because of insufficient funds clear the second time they are deposited. Notify the customer that his or her account is overdrawn and that you are redepositing the check. If the check is returned a second time, inquire about the policies of your bank – in some areas, a bank will not allow you to redeposit a check after a second return for insufficient funds. When a bad check becomes your collection problem, you can try sending the check writer a notice by registered mail, like the one on page 144, along with a copy of the check plus details of your state's laws against the passage of bad checks.

If the notice brings no response, follow-up phone calls may prove more effective. Failing that, your next step might involve one of the following four options.

1. Ask your bank to put the check on "collection" status. Your bank will return the bad check to the issuer's bank, and when sufficient funds are collected in the issuer's account, the check will receive priority payment.

2. If this attempt proves unsuccessful, you can contact your local police department and protest the check. You will be asked to complete certain forms that must be approved by the issuer's bank, and the police will issue a warrant for the issuer's arrest.

3. If the police determine that the size of the check does not merit their pursuit of the case, your company's attorney can file a civil complaint. A subpoena will be issued and a court date set.

4. As a last resort, you can turn the matter over to a collection agency. The rates charged by collection agencies usually are based on a large percentage of the amount they collect.

No Account

A check returned by the bank and marked "no account" usually is evidence of fraud unless there has been an extraordinary error. In rare instances, a customer may issue a check on the wrong bank or on a discontinued account. Determine quickly what the circumstances are, and proceed with your collection efforts.

Closed Account

A check marked "closed account" is a sign of extreme carelessness or fraud. Accounts are closed by both individuals and banks. A bank may close an account because of too many overdrafts, or an individual may open a new account and forget that he or she has issued a check that is still outstanding against the old account. Again, determine the circumstances of the individual case, and proceed with collection or prosecution efforts.

NOTICE OF RETURNED CHECK

Dear Customer:

You will find outlined below information relating to your check recently returned to us unhonored. We realize the complexity of keeping accurate bank balances and know that you would like to honor your check. We appreciate your business and are sorry for the inconvenience.

10 day
NOTICE   **RETURNED CHECK INFORMATION**   10 day
NOTICE

You are hereby notified that your check dated ⎯⎯⎯⎯⎯ 19⎯, for $⎯⎯⎯⎯ has been presented to the bank for payment and has been returned to us unpaid. Please arrange to pay the amount of this check within ten (10) business days from the date you first receive this notice.

Date ⎯⎯⎯⎯⎯⎯⎯⎯   ⎯⎯⎯⎯⎯⎯⎯⎯ (Store)
Signed ⎯⎯⎯⎯⎯⎯⎯   ⎯⎯⎯⎯⎯⎯⎯ (Address)
Phone ⎯⎯⎯⎯⎯⎯⎯   ⎯⎯⎯⎯⎯⎯ (Town, State)

(PLACE CHECK HERE WHEN COPYING)

**[Quote your state's law or penal code
against the passage of bad checks]**

IMPORTANT – Please make your check good within 10 days! **If you fail to honor your check within 10 days after receiving this notice we will be forced to consider appropriate legal action.**

Forgery

Forged checks are worthless – a total loss to your business. When you suspect an individual is attempting to pass a bad check in your store or business:

- Attempt to stall the suspect without arousing suspicion.

- Call the police immediately.

- When the police arrive, let them interrogate the suspect, and follow their instructions.

- If the suspect flees before the police arrive, try to make note of a description of the suspect and any companions, the license number and a physical description of the car or other vehicle used, and the direction taken.

In Cases of Fraud

When you find that you have accepted a fraudulent check, contact your local police department. Some retail establishments also may want to notify their local Chamber of Commerce and their central security office to alert other stores in the area and other branches of their own business. Also keep in mind these tips from the Small Business Administration:

- **You cannot prosecute bad-check passers without strong evidence.** Place the check in a sealed envelope and handle it as little as possible. Attempt to positively identify the check writer and to connect him or her with the receiving of money or merchandise for the bad check.

- **Be willing to prosecute.** Businesses with a reputation for being tough on bad-check passers are less likely to be victimized.

- **Any alteration, illegal signature, forgery of the endorsement, or erasure or obliteration on a genuine check is a crime.** Issuing a bad check to pay for merchandise is not a theft but a misdemeanor, which carries a lighter penalty than a theft. The passing of a bad out-of-state check is a federal offense – contact your local branch of the FBI, listed in your phone directory. Forged U.S. Government checks should be referred to the U.S. Secret Service (see Appendix A).

CHAPTER 13

Coupon Fraud

THE CASE OF
The Free Lunch

Every day a number of different discount coupons are presented by customers at a fast-food restaurant and are redeemed for food. When coupons clipped from locally distributed coupon books begin appearing, the store manager redeems them and stacks them with the others. At the end of the month, the dollar value of all the coupons is tabulated, and they are mailed to the restaurant chain's headquarters for credit.

A week later the store manager receives a telephone call from headquarters. The coupons clipped from the locally distributed books were not authorized by the company and appear to be counterfeit. Even the "guaranteed redemption" offer printed on the back of the coupons has been falsified. Contacting local law enforcement officials, the store owner learns that his was only one of a number of area businesses that accepted counterfeit coupons. Fast-talking con artists apparently printed fictitious coupon books offering discounts at several hundred area businesses and then sold the books in bulk and at a discount to area religious and social groups. Those unwitting accomplices handled the marketing and sales.

And, of course, by the time the coupons began appearing at area retail establishments and the scheme was uncovered, the culprits had long since left town.

Couponing: a $3.5 Billion Business

To the average consumer, couponing represents a means of shaving a few dollars off the weekly grocery bill or enjoying an evening out at a reduced price. To retailers, couponing offers a way to revive business during a slow period or attract new customers. To companies manufacturing a product or providing a service, couponing is a time-tested method for introducing new products or services, or spurring sales. In any case, couponing today saves consumers over $3.5 billion annually, and that figure is growing daily.

When most consumers hear the word couponing, they think of those 25¢ or 50¢ discount coupons that appear in newspapers, magazines, and direct mail packets. But in the 1980s and 1990s, couponing has expanded dramatically. It is no longer unusual to receive coupons worth $50 or $100 off the purchase of a major appliance or even several hundred dollars off the purchase of a new car.

Because coupons are redeemable for money, large blocks of misredeemed (credited against purchases that never occur) or counterfeit coupons can cost an advertiser or retailer thousands of dollars each month. And when coupons fall into the wrong hands, they don't stimulate the sales of products or services as intended. Thus, the damage is doubly expensive.

According to industry representatives, the hardest-hit victims of coupon fraud activities are product manufacturers. In most cases, it is the manufacturer who ends up paying for

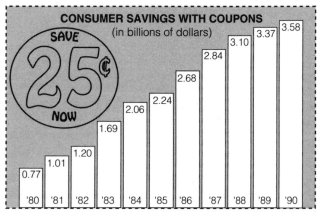

CONSUMER SAVINGS WITH COUPONS (in billions of dollars)

'80	'81	'82	'83	'84	'85	'86	'87	'88	'89	'90
0.77	1.01	1.20	1.69	2.06	2.24	2.68	2.84	3.10	3.37	3.58

Source : NCH Promotional Services

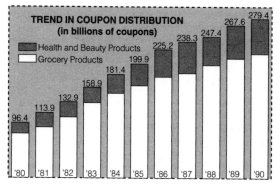

TREND IN COUPON DISTRIBUTION
(in billions of coupons)

■ Health and Beauty Products
□ Grocery Products

96.4 113.9 132.9 158.9 181.4 199.9 225.2 238.3 247.4 267.6 279.4

'80 '81 '82 '83 '84 '85 '86 '87 '88 '89 '90

Source: NCH Promotional Services

fraudulently redeemed coupons. However, with greater numbers of local merchants distributing their own coupons, swindlers increasingly are targeting these smaller, more susceptible merchants.

How Couponing and Coupon Fraud Work

In its most basic form, a coupon is a written offer of a discounted or free product or service. A legitimate coupon will contain the terms of the offer and inform retailers that the issuer of the coupon will reimburse them for its face value.

Coupons are normally issued to prospective customers by the manufacturer of a product or provider of a service. The coupon may be redeemed, or bought back, from the consumer by the retailer selling that product or service. The majority of coupons are then sent by the retailer to a clearinghouse rather than directly to the manufacturer or service provider. The clearinghouse sorts the different coupons, counts them, and tabulates their value. It then reimburses the retailer for the total value of coupons received. The clearinghouse ships the canceled coupons to the various manufacturers, who in turn pay the clearinghouse the face value of the coupons plus a handling charge for its services.

Because the redemption process involves so many different participating groups, there are numerous opportunities for coupon fraud. Among the most common abuses are:

• The sale of newspaper coupon inserts by newspaper employees.

- The interception and sale of direct mail coupons by postal workers.

- The redemption by retailers of coupons for purchases of merchandise other than that specified by the manufacturers and the subsequent submission of those coupons to the manufacturers for reimbursement.

- The submission of illegally obtained coupons by clearing-houses to manufacturers.

- The production of counterfeit coupons and their submission singly to local retailers or in bulk to clearinghouses.

HOW TO PROTECT YOUR BUSINESS

Couponing experts urge businesses that use coupons in their promotions to learn as much as possible about the people or businesses that will be involved in distributing their coupons. Among the questions that should be addressed are:

- How are coupons or preprinted advertising inserts stored?

- Is there a security system to guard coupons or inserts against theft?

- What is the distribution process?

- How is theft by those distributing the coupons or inserts prevented?

- Are coupons or inserts that have not been distributed returned to the printer or advertiser? If so, what security precautions are taken?

- What is done with undistributed coupons or inserts that are not returned? Are they destroyed? If so, under what guidelines and security procedures?

With these questions in mind, be alert for distributors who show indications of:

- Little or no apparent security in the storage of coupons or inserts.

- A poorly supervised or undocumented distribution and/or mailing system.

- Lack of a clear-cut procedure for recovering or accounting for undistributed coupons or inserts.

- No periodic checking system to determine whether coupons or inserts are distributed and disposed of properly.

While it may be difficult for the average businessperson to detect or prevent coupon fraud, the first line of defense is an informed skepticism. If you are approached by someone offering a dubious plan, don't become involved until you are certain that it is a legitimate business arrangement. For example, don't let anyone persuade you that it is a regular course of business to sell coupons in bulk to another person or business at a discounted price – the only transfers of money in couponing should take place between the consumer and the retailer and between the retailer and the advertiser or its clearinghouse.

Also remember that your business is not required to accept coupons that you suspect are counterfeit. Counterfeit coupons usually are poorly printed copies of the originals, with the printing in one color and on one side only. Legitimate coupons should give the name and address of the manufacturer, an expiration date or indication that there is none, and a description of redemption guidelines. Businesses that use coupons in their promotions can make the counterfeiter's job more difficult by issuing coupons that contain all these elements and are printed on both sides and in at least two colors.

Newspaper Industry Guidelines

The Audit Bureau of Circulations, an organization of advertisers, advertising agencies, and newspaper and periodical publishers, recommends that businesses using newspapers for coupon or insert distribution insist on the newspapers' compliance with the following industry guidelines:

1. When inserts are provided by the business, the paper should verify that:

   - The number of inserts received matches the number shipped.

   - Inserts are placed in a secure area until removed by authorized personnel.

   - Inserts are placed in the newspaper for distribution according to the agreement.

   - Leftover inserts are disposed of in a manner that makes them unusable for redemption.

2. When the newspaper prints the inserts, its circulation department should verify that:
   - Pressroom reports or statements list the number of sections run for each issue.

- Spoiled coupon sections and sections remaining after printing and insertion are disposed of in a manner that makes them unusable for redemption.
- Coupon sections printed prior to the date of insertion are placed in a secure area until removed by authorized personnel for insertion in the newspaper.
- Printing plates or other material used to print coupon sections are disposed of properly.

3. When the coupon or insert distribution is completed, you should ask the newspaper's circulation department for:

- Auditable records or statements to confirm the disposition of returns, leftovers, and unsold copies from employees, distributors, carriers, drivers, and others responsible for the recovery and destruction of newspapers containing advertiser coupons.
- Statements from wastepaper companies or other firms that purchase newspaper copies containing advertising coupons that coupons are disposed of in a manner that makes them unusable for redemption.

WHAT TO DO IF YOU ARE VICTIMIZED

If you have been the victim of coupon fraud, a number of federal and state laws may have been violated. If the fraud involves the counterfeit reproduction of coupons, federal laws involving counterfeiting and trademark and copyright laws may have bearing. If the fraud involves transactions by the U.S. mail, a number of postal fraud laws may come into play.

The first step a manufacturer or other coupon issuer should take when fraud has occurred is to stop payment on any questionable coupon redemptions. If the alleged fraud involves possible misredemption on the part of another business or franchise, the manufacturer should demand proof of purchase.

If the U.S. mail has been involved, contact local U.S. Postal authorities or the Chief Postal Inspector, U.S. Postal Service (see Appendix A), and ask for an investigation of potential coupon fraud. The Postal Service will in turn contact your local U.S. attorney general's office and ask for an indictment, if warranted. You should also contact the state attorney general's office, listed in your telephone directory.

In addition, report the fraud to your local Better Business Bureau (see Appendix B). The BBB will include the information in its files to alert future inquirers.

CHAPTER 14

Cargo Theft

THE CASE OF
The Wheeler-Dealers

A major food wholesaler services hundreds of grocery stores in a tristate area. Thousands of cartons of boxed and canned food are delivered every week by the wholesaler's fleet of tractor-trailer trucks, and because of the large volume of shipments, a certain percentage of losses through ruptured cartons, broken glass containers, and otherwise damaged or misplaced merchandise is built into costs.

When the accounting department decides to take a close look at these losses, it discovers that a large majority can be attributed to three of the drivers. Contacting the managers of the groceries serviced by those drivers, accounting further discovers that, for a number of the stores, short deliveries are a small but recurring problem. The wholesaler hires a private detective firm to discreetly investigate the problem.

Several weeks of observation and inquiry reveal that the three inventive drivers have come up with a simple plan for supplementing their income. By short-shipping their regular customers, they are able to make deliveries to several small, private groceries that pay for the cartons of food in cash. The drivers pocket the money and report to their employer that the missing cartons were damaged and discarded in transit or that their trucks were shorted at the loading dock.

The dishonest drivers are turned over to the police. The lost revenues, which over a three-year period have amounted to more than one hundred thousand dollars, are never recovered.

Cargo Theft:
Ten-billion-dollar Annual Losses

About ten billion dollars are lost annually through cargo theft, according to the National Cargo Security Council. Most cargo theft occurs in freight-handling areas. The thieves may be customers working in collusion with shipping company employees, highway bandits who rob delivery vehicles in transit, department workers employed by the shipping company or by an independent shipper hired to handle distribution, or truck drivers or others involved in the delivery process. But most often they are employees. In fact, as much as 90 percent of all cargo losses may be attributed to collusion.

HOW TO PROTECT YOUR BUSINESS

Given the high level of employee complicity, the keystone of any security program is careful preemployment screening. A thorough preemployment check includes examining the backgrounds of prospects with an eye to work experience, arrests and convictions, and credit history.

A chronological look at the steps involved in the shipment of cargo points out the areas of opportunity for crime – and the steps businesses can take at each stage to thwart the criminals.

1. **The shipping process begins when an authorized employee or manager fills out or signs orders approving the shipment of merchandise to another company.**

   An unauthorized shipment begins in the same way, but in this case, no legitimate order has been placed and the merchandise may be shipped to a drop-off point selected by the employee. The evidence of illegal activity is camouflaged by either destroying or altering invoices or shipping instructions. In a fraudulent overshipment, excess goods are shipped and subsequently sold by an accomplice at the receiving end.

   Problems are more prevalent in companies that do not investigate or require the return of overshipped merchandise. A strictly controlled ordering and invoicing system is an important first step in reducing the risk of unauthorized shipments. Ideally, all sales tickets should be numbered and these numbers and the sales they represent logged at least once a week in a sales register. Spoiled, mismarked, or canceled sales tickets should be clearly marked "VOID" and turned over to an authorized billing clerk.

Some businesses find the use of a sales receipt register helpful in encouraging salespeople to keep careful and complete records. These machines "crank out" prenumbered sales tickets and automatically "crank forward" copies of completed sales tickets into a sealed compartment, access to which should be limited to an authorized billing clerk.

Customer invoices should be handled in a similarly controlled, numbered fashion, and sealed invoice registers, with access to the secured copies limited to authorized accounting personnel, may be a valuable precaution.

If possible, products also should be numbered, either individually or in crates, and the numbers corresponding to the products recorded on the sales ticket, shipping instructions, and invoice. These numbers can then be checked against inventory records by the auditing or accounting department.

2. **The merchandise is assembled and packaged for transit – commonly called the staging process.**

Theft at this stage of shipment is often made possible by disorganization. The most crime-ridden assembly areas are those in which employee and customer access are not controlled, products are not arranged in an organized manner, and sound inventory control procedures are not followed. Dishonest employees and customers may take advantage of the lack of order by walking off with merchandise or concealing it for later removal.

Careful planning and organization can virtually eliminate theft during the staging process. The assembly and packaging of goods for shipment should always take place in an area specifically set aside for that purpose, such as a warehouse or packaging plant – *never* at a loading dock or similar area where merchandise is readily visible and accessible to employees and customers. Access to the staging area should be limited to assigned employees and should be watched over by a manager or security guard. Inventory control should be required at every stage of the process. A sound inventory control system might operate in the following manner:

- *Sales tickets* are handed to an employee solely responsible for pulling the merchandise from stock. That employee writes the product registration or inventory number on the sales ticket. Some warehouses attach a removable inventory control number to every item, which is removed from the carton and attached to the sales ticket. When the order has been filled, the employee initials the sales ticket and passes it on to:

- *A second employee,* who is responsible for checking the merchandise against the sales ticket, initialing the sales ticket, and packaging the merchandise. That employee then passes on the sales ticket to:

- *The accounting department,* which records the inventory control numbers in an inventory register.

Employees involved in the assembly and packaging process should be regularly rotated from their assignments. A member of management should periodically oversee the staging procedure to ensure its proper execution and should examine shipments at random to verify that orders are being filled properly.

3. **Merchandise is loaded onto trucks for transit.**

The loading process can provide dishonest employees and customers with fertile opportunities for theft. In poorly controlled operations where customers and employees are permitted to congregate in the loading area, cargo can easily be carried off and concealed in waiting trucks or cars. *Short packaging* is another common loading dock crime. Employees divert a truck driver's attention long enough to slip packages away from the driver's shipment, and the driver then signs the delivery receipt, acknowledging that he has verified the count of the shipment. Usually the driver does not realize he has been shortchanged until after his delivery. At that stage, he is held responsible for the shortage.

Precautions similar to those used to limit access and control activities in the staging area also can be effective in preventing theft in the cargo area.

- Limit access to authorized personnel and vehicles. Trucks should not be permitted to approach the loading platform until they are ready to be loaded, and drivers should not be allowed behind the receiving fence.

- One employee should be made responsible for overseeing each transaction or shipment. That employee should initial the delivery receipt, thereby verifying that the proper merchandise has left the loading dock.

- If possible, one employee should handle the physical transfer of the merchandise, and another, preferably a member of management, should oversee the accuracy of the transaction.

- Employees should be periodically rotated in their assignments. The drivers, or whoever picks up the merchandise, should be required to examine the shipment and sign the delivery receipt.

4. **The merchandise is transported by truck or tractor-trailer to the point of delivery.**

   Theft directly from delivery vehicles may involve the pilferage of small, costly items from a shipment, commonly called tailgate theft, or robbery by force of the entire contents of a truck.

   Before the shipment leaves the store or warehouse, its contents should be listed on a roster, with copies provided to the company selling the merchandise, the delivery company (if different), the receiving company, and the driver. When the contents are loaded and in transit, observe the following precautions:

- Keep merchandise under lock and key at all times.

- Where theft is likely, avoid the use of flatbed trucks that make merchandise visible and accessible.

- Loaded vehicles that are parked overnight should be locked so that the delivery doors cannot be opened, for example, back to back.

- The parking area should be well lit, and, where possible, guarded. Some large truck stops provide protected areas for a reasonable fee.

- Avoid parking loaded delivery vehicles in high-risk areas, such as inner cities.
- Alarms should be installed in delivery vehicles, particularly those that often must be parked overnight when full of merchandise.
- Schedules should be arranged so that, whenever possible, shipments can be made without overnight stops.
- When a shipment requires the use of more than one vehicle or when several vehicles are heading in the same direction, they should travel together in a convoy.
- A security guard in a separate vehicle should follow shipments of particularly high value or risk.
- Information on shipment contents, departure and arrival times, and route plans should be kept confidential.
- Radio or telephone communication devices should be installed in all delivery vehicles.
- The company's name, address, and telephone number should be marked on all sides of delivery vehicles so that police can quickly identify stolen vehicles.

WHAT TO DO IF YOU ARE VICTIMIZED

Cargo theft should be handled like any other form of theft. If you observe an employee or customer in the process of committing the crime, contact your local police department immediately. Try to detain the suspect as long as possible *without using force* and, if possible, without arousing suspicion. If the suspect leaves the premises before the police arrive, have ready a detailed description of the suspect and any companions, and, if possible, the license number and description of the suspect's car or other vehicle. Also try to make note of the direction the suspect takes when leaving. Any further investigation should be left to the police.

If cargo theft occurs in transit, immediately contact local police authorities. State police should also be provided with a detailed description of stolen merchandise and, if possible, of the suspects and getaway vehicle.

If the police determine that the interstate transfer of stolen goods is involved, the FBI also should be notified (see Appendix A).

CHAPTER 15

Industrial Espionage

THE CASE OF
The Suspect Supervisor

Top sales executives at a large U.S.-based electronics firm can't believe their bad luck. They've just learned that a competitor has been selected for a large government contract – and the rival's winning bid was just $600 less than their own price. A review of bids and contracts over the past three years reveals that two competitors have consistently underbid the firm, often by just a few thousand dollars.

Agreement is reached to bring in an outside security consultant. The investigative firm hired concurs with managements' suspicions: Pricing is somehow being leaked to competitors. A discreet sweep is made of the executive offices and conference rooms, but no hidden microphones or tape recorders are found. Further investigation begins to focus on the firm's pricing supervisor, an employee with over fifteen years of service and a lifestyle more luxurious than his $60,000-a-year salary would seem to support. In an undercover operation conducted by the investigator, the supervisor is finally nabbed in the act of sending, via computer, what he believes is a confidential bid to one of the rival firms.

The electronics firm estimates that it has lost dozens of contracts and perhaps millions of dollars due to the collusion between this trusted employee and the owners of its two top competitors. The employee eventually is sentenced to a short prison term and a $10,000 fine; the case against the rival firms drags on for years.

Corporate Gold Miners

Corporate electronic theft by industrial spies and disloyal employees costs American businesses billions of dollars in missed sales and wasted research and development costs each year. Further, government security experts maintain that the theft of business data by foreign spies from hostile nations as well as allies is eating away at this nation's competitive advantage.

The growth in information crimes is largely a result of the rising value of information in our increasingly technological world. Trade secrets are the new gold of today's marketplace. Mining that gold are a new generation of information pirates ranging from rank amateurs equipped with relatively inexpensive microwave receivers to private corporate intelligence experts armed with an arsenal of electronic eavesdropping tools.

The specialty of these corporate spies is silent crime. Many companies, in fact, never know they have been victimized – a firm may be well aware that it has lost out on a few contracts but completely unaware that the winning bid was submitted by a rival in possession of its marketing plans, manufacturing secrets, and negotiating strategies.

Virtually no secret is safe from the determined corporate spy. In the battle for competitive intelligence, U.S. businesses large and small have fallen victim over the past few years to a variety of industrial espionage schemes.

Employee Leaks

According to some security experts, the greatest threat to a corporation's trade secrets is its own employees, past and present. Information can slip out innocently, through executives, salespeople, and suppliers, or disgruntled current or former employees can steal proprietary data to sell to competitive firms. Some corporate moles do their work undetected for years. One company in the aviation and aerospace industry found in the 1980s that it had lost millions of dollars due to the actions of a single employee with access to pricing; over a five-year period that employee had sold thousands of advance bids to competitors, enabling them to underbid his own employer.

More blatant but just as difficult to combat are the so-called "brain drain" cases, in which competitors hire away a company's top executives to gain access to top level trade secrets.

Purloined Papers

It doesn't take a degree in electronics or even a rudimentary understanding of the workings of the microphone to launch a career as a corporate spy. Trade secrets are often as close, and as easy to transport, as the papers on an executive's desk – or in the trash can.

Long before computers became a common fixture of the workplace, formulas, blueprints, marketing plans, customer lists, and other proprietary documents found their way from originator to competitor, with the help of a company employee or an outside thief. In 1989, an American automaker discovered, in the pages of a trade magazine, high-quality photos of a top secret auto that it had planned to unveil the next year at a cost of some three billion dollars. The company believed the photos were leaked by an employee in its design studio. That employee had an easier task than the private detectives hired in 1991 by a cosmetics company. The investigators were instructed to dig up information to help the company fight off a takeover bid by a competitive firm. In what corporate investigators say is a widespread and, in most cases, entirely legal practice, the industrious investigators sifted for information among the trash in the competitor's parking lot dumpster.

Electronic Espionage

Any secret transmitted over the air can be pirated, according to security experts, with the theft virtually impossible to detect. Here's a look at a few of the tools in the industrial spy's bag of tricks:

- **Microphones and tape recorders** can and have been concealed anywhere top secret conversations take place – in the ceilings of conference rooms, high-level executives' offices, even in executive washrooms. Bugging an office, however, is more difficult to do and less commonly done than tapping a phone line.

- **Telephone tapping** is one of the most common forms of electronic eavesdropping. Often a spy posing as a telephone repairperson gains easy access to a company's offices and phone lines. The tapper either cuts and taps into the phone line or simply places a "noninvasive" bug next to the phone wire, where its transmitter can broadcast conversations via radio frequencies to a listener or tape recorder. Car-phone bugs have grown increasingly common over the past few years with the growth of the cellular phone industry.

- **Fax tapping** is a form of phone bugging. Fax transmissions are doubly vulnerable, however, since they make use of the easily corrupted telephone lines and result in two equally purloinable hard copies.

- **Telex transmissions** are similarly vulnerable. The bid you telex to a prospective client overseas may well find its way into a foreign competitor's machine as well.

- **Aerial spying** absolves the industrial snoop from criminal trespass charges, and it can be an effective means of gathering information on the physical layout of a competitor's manufacturing operations.

- **New electronic eavesdropping devices** are constantly being developed. Some of the more exotic gadgets include a laser gun that measures sound vibrations in an office window to pick up conversations up to a half-mile away; binoculars that both see and hear, with a receiver capable of zeroing in on conversations within a five-block radius; and an electronic bug disguised as, well, a bug. Many of these increasingly sophisticated gadgets find their way into local electronics stores.

Computer Espionage

Anyone who knows how to use a personal computer can access any information stored in it. Computer hackers intent on espionage use a variety of techniques, from casually perusing a spreadsheet carelessly left on a screen during a coffee break, to physically breaking into a company's or government agency's offices to access classified information stored in its computers, to using sophisticated listening devices. Those high-tech devices include, for example, electronic eavesdroppers that can tap into electromagnetic waves to intercept information from a computer screen or printer as much as a mile away.

Information Seekers Abroad

Intelligence experts have known for decades what U.S. businesses have only begun to acknowledge: Foreign governments routinely acquire intelligence information on American firms and share it with their own businesses. The employees of foreign corporations often do their own digging as well. Information acquisition can take a fairly innocuous form. For example, in the case of the corporate executive who socializes with an American competitor and later sends his home office extensive notes on the American's family, life-style, and interests. Or it can take the far more dangerous form of the government that recruits spies in U.S. electronics firms to pass along research, manufacturing, marketing, and negotiating secrets.

In the past few years, security officials have uncovered foreign intelligence espionage cases including:

☐ A major espionage program run by a U.S. ally, in which industrial intelligence-gathering techniques included the recruiting of moles inside U.S. firms, the interception of electronic messages, and hotel room break-ins during which copies were made of documents left behind by businesspeople traveling abroad.

☐ A large U.S. equipment maker that was consistently underbid by a foreign rival, until a private investigator discovered that the foreign firm was bribing an employee of the U.S. company to obtain advance bid information.

☐ A major U.S. food processor that was forced to close its main plant to public tours when it learned that spies from two foreign competitors had collected valuable information while visiting the plant.

It does not appear that U.S. firms will benefit any time soon from the kind of information sharing that takes place in other countries. But many U.S. national security experts caution that, unless American firms take stronger measures to recognize and counter foreign industrial espionage, they will continue to operate at a competitive disadvantage.

Corporations storing client lists, access codes, financial data, and other confidential information on computers are becoming increasingly concerned over the threat of computer tapping.

Computer crime is explored at length in chapter nineteen, with some of the techniques used by computer tappers outlined on pages 197 to 201 and the steps businesses can take to combat computer eavesdropping detailed on pages 201 to 205.

HOW TO PROTECT YOUR BUSINESS

American corporations are spending more money than ever on tracking their competitors, according to the Conference Board, a business-funded research organization. Most competitive intelligence is gathered by entirely legal and ethical means, such as training employees to be alert to useful information; asking the right questions of suppliers, customers, and even the competition; reviewing publicly available tax information, blueprints, labor contracts, and other useful documents; and benchmarking – taking apart a rival's product or service and analyzing it piece by piece with an eye to improving each component. At the same time, companies are waking up to the need to do more to protect their own sensitive information from prying eyes and ears. Here are some of the tools and techniques corporations can use to foil information thieves:

1. **Education.** Employees should be alerted to the serious consequences of leaking sensitive information. That includes being wary of so-called consulting firms that may call to ask questions as part of an "industry study," and of headhunting firms that may have been hired by a competitor to tap into company secrets by interviewing unsuspecting employees. Employees also should be warned to be wary at conferences, trade shows, and hospitality suites. According to one prominent attorney and industrial security consultant, these events are where much corporate snooping takes place and where "many a trade secret has been divulged over a drink." That attorney also advises inserting a statement in job application forms specifying that the applicant understands and voluntarily complies with your company's trade secret protection guidelines.

2. **Background checks.** It's wise to do a thorough check on all prospective employees, especially those who will handle sensitive overseas assignments.

3. **Document disposal.** Sensitive papers should be destroyed or shredded before disposal. However even that may not be enough to deter the determined corporate spy. It's not uncommon for "dumpster raiders" to gather and then painstakingly piece together shredded documents. If you believe your company's trash may look tempting to a rival, your best recourse may simply be to beef up security near the dumpster.

4. **Conduct a "sting."** If you suspect but are not certain that a competitor is eavesdropping, a simple ruse may answer the question. One private security expert recommends sending your branch office a cable, telex, or fax containing phony information, such as notification of a price increase. If a rival responds by raising its own prices, you know further investigation and countermeasures are in order.

5. **Electronic countermeasures.** As electronic eavesdropping devices become increasingly sophisticated, the number and complexity of electronic countermeasures keeps pace. Electronic devices can alert you to the presence of phone taps, concealed tape recorders, and other silent snoops, and many are small and portable enough to be used by traveling executives to debug a car or hotel room.

Several firms specialize in providing electronic countermeasure devices to corporate security departments and business executives. Among the high-tech gadgets designed to foil the eavesdropper are:

- Voltage detectors, or "tap alerts," which detect deviations from the normal voltage of a telephone line, thus warning of the presence of an invasive phone tap.

- Spectrum analyzers, which search the air for the pulses broadcast by most noninvasive listening devices over radio frequencies. These bug detectors can be small enough to conceal in a shirt pocket, and some silently vibrate or light up to warn you when you are in the presence of a hidden transmitter.

- Encryption devices, which can be used to scramble communications going out over car phones, broadcast satellites, telexes, and fax machines. Many work by automatically encoding communications and decoding them at the other end through a paired scrambler. Or, as in the case of most fax encrypters, operators at both ends have access to the same secret key, or password, which enables the machine to encode and decode the transmission.

6. **Computer security.** The most important weapon of most corporate intelligence gatherers is the computer. See pages 201 to 205 for tips on tightening computer security.

7. **Security consultants.** Private investigators specializing in corporate intelligence are enjoying a booming business. These corporate private eyes offer services such as:

- Performing detailed background checks on prospective employees, board members, and business partners.
- Debugging a company's offices – searching for sources of information leaks and advising appropriate countermeasures.
- Gathering financial information and other background intelligence on competitors. For example, during corporate takeover battles, in which sensitive and possibly unfavorable information about a suitor can help management respond to the threat.

One way to find a good private investigator is to ask for referrals from a trusted attorney or insurance executive who is in charge of a claims department. When hiring an investigator, make sure he or she has expertise in your specific area of concern, spell out exactly what you want done and in what time frame, ask for an estimate of costs, insist on itemized billing, and, unless your lawyer advises otherwise, get the agreement in writing.

WHAT TO DO IF YOU ARE VICTIMIZED

According to many industrial intelligence experts, the U.S. legal system has not yet adapted to the new mode of crime practiced by information thieves. While some states have enacted legislation designed to help companies prosecute trade secret pirates, in far too many cases outdated laws allow these criminals to slip through the cracks.

State and federal law enforcers often are too busy to invest the time and manpower to gather the evidence needed to prove the theft of trade secrets. Further, some judges are reluctant to enforce restrictions that might give one company the edge over another. Victimized companies are left with few options. Some major corporations have adopted an aggressive policy in bringing information pirates to court, filing and vigorously pursuing theft-of-information suits against unethical competitors. Many have been frustrated in attempting to protect secrets by these legal means, but some have been able to force competitors to pay penalties or produce their products for inspection. And some corporations have found that the government is more receptive to taking legal action when the company collects the evidence of crime itself, through its own intelligence-gathering operation or a private detective agency.

When your company is victimized by an information thief, your most important response is a willingness to report the crime and prosecute the offenders. The first step is to gather all the facts and take the matter to the local police department. Care must be taken to stay strictly within the law when assembling evidence. If corporate staffers do not have the expertise to properly gather and protect evidence, you might consider hiring an outside security consultant or private detective. Some companies provide incentives, such as cash bonuses, to employees for information that can be used in identifying and prosecuting information thieves.

The police and your attorney can help you to determine what laws have been violated and whether the crime committed against your business comes under the jurisdiction of federal agencies. If your case goes to court, be prepared to show that the money and resources you have invested in developing and protecting the stolen information make the theft a bona fide crime rather than just a business setback. Remember, your wisest and most effective response may well be to put effective countermeasures in place to prevent further losses. Again, an outside security consultant may provide valuable assistance, and an experienced consultant may even be able to help you pinpoint what the information thief was trying to learn by spying on your company, thus enabling you to benefit from identifying your competition's weaknesses.

SECTION III

 INTERNAL CRIME

CHAPTER 16

Pilferage and Embezzlement

 ## THE CASE OF
The Cooked Books

The controller for a small retail operation seems an exemplary, practically indispensable employee. The woman started in accounts receivable when the store first opened ten years ago, and today she is solely responsible for handling billing, accounts receivable, audits, and customer complaints. Rarely taking a day off and never a full week's vacation, she has always impressed fellow workers and company owners with her hard work and dedication.

The controller has reaped the rewards of her labors. She owns an impressive home, a weekend cottage, and new cars every other year. No one has ever questioned her ability to afford these niceties – until the time she becomes ill and is hospitalized and the owners are forced to take over her financial responsibilities.

Several customer complaints about inaccurate billings raise troubling questions and prompt a careful examination of the records – an examination that gradually uncovers the elements of a meticulously planned scheme that for years has been allowing the controller to secretly embezzle thousands of dollars from company profits. A key facet of her scheme involves the regular pocketing of all or a portion of cash payments on open accounts and the altering of company records and subsequent invoices to acknowledge receipt of lesser sums. Because she has been in charge of all aspects of the company's billing and record keeping, the controller, has been able to successfully accomplish and camouflage this and other deceptions.

While the woman is eventually tried and found guilty of embezzlement, the company will never completely recuperate from the loss of revenues.

Crimes of Confidence

Dishonest employees account for an estimated two-thirds of all retail theft, according to the Small Business Administration, with retail theft losses from all sources ranging from about 1.3 percent of sales for a well-managed store to 7 percent for the loosely controlled organization.

Pilferage and embezzlement are the most common types of employee theft, with pilferage the more prevalent of the two. While both crimes involve deception by employees, they differ in the level of trust accorded employees by their employers. Pilferage more often is carried out by lower-level employees, while employees with access to cash and/or records, subject to fewer controls, and better able to circumvent procedures, engage in embezzlement.

 ## HOW TO PROTECT YOUR BUSINESS

Pilferage

The theft of a company's goods and commodities by its employees, or pilferage, does not require the altering of a company's financial records and is usually carried out by employees who have access to merchandise but little or no access to company records or bookkeeping.

The many techniques used by pilfering employees include concealing merchandise inside clothing or packages; using products directly from a retail store's shelves; hiding merchandise in trash receptacles for pickup at a later time; purposely breaking or damaging products, reporting the damage, and taking the "worthless" merchandise home; conspiring with delivery people or employees of a company doing business with one's employer to remove merchandise from the premises; replacing a container full of merchandise with an empty or partially full container; and running personal mail through the company postage meter.

Most pilferers are otherwise honest individuals who probably don't think of themselves as thieves. Strategically posted diplomatic reminders telling employees that pilferage erodes the funds that otherwise could go into wages, benefits, and company growth can help reduce the incidence of pilferage by such individuals. Other preventive measures should aim at removing both temptation and opportunity. A clear-cut policy that outlines acceptable working procedures and details the company's approach to pilferage might include some of the following guidelines. These steps are not appropriate for all businesses, but where they are observed, they should prove effective deterrents.

1. **All prospective employees should be carefully screened.** A conscientious reference check on all new employees can help you avoid costly hiring mistakes.

2. **Owners-managers should avoid setting a double standard of moral and ethical conduct.** If an employee sees a supervisor in even a minor dishonest act, he or she is encouraged in the same direction. Set reasonable rules, enforce them rigidly, consistently, and apply them equally to everyone.

3. **All employees should be required to enter and leave the workplace through designated employee entrances** that are watched over by a security guard or management personnel. A coatroom should be provided for overcoats and unusually large packages. Toolboxes, packages, and other containers carried by exiting employees should be inspected by a supervisor or guard.

4. **Central station alarm systems, motion detectors, or electric eyes should be used to protect the workplace after hours.** These can put the "break-out-artist" – the employee who hides and then leaves the premises after closing – out of commission.

5. **Access to supply areas should be restricted** and should be watched over by a security guard or kept under lock and key. Employees who enter the supply area should be accompanied by a warehouse employee. Names, times of entrance and departure, and merchandise removed should be noted on a sign-in sheet.

6. **Stockroom merchandise** should be kept in neat stacks rather than disorderly piles, so that it is easy to spot when items are missing. Merchandise on display for sale also should be kept in neat, orderly displays and should never be stacked near opening windows or doors.

7. **Company equipment should be clearly marked with the company's name** and tools should be inventoried and locked up by a supervisor at the end of each workday. Be suspicious when company equipment or merchandise appears to be out of place. Encourage employees to report out-of-place items to management. Insist that all padlocks be fastened when not in use to prevent lock switching, and control access to keys.

8. **Product components used on assembly lines should be inventoried and kept in secure areas.** Only the amount of material required for each day's production should be removed from the secured area.

9. **Employees of one department should be rotated to a different department for taking inventory,** or inventory taking should be supervised by a member of management. Security guards should be routinely rotated, too, in order to discourage complacency and fraternization.

10. **Shipping and receiving activities should be based in separate areas of a company's facilities.** Only merchandise authorized for shipment should be permitted in the shipping area, and a security guard should be posted to ensure that no merchandise leaves the premises through the receiving area. Incoming shipments should be double-checked to prevent collusion between dishonest drivers and receiving department employees. (Also see Chapter 14, "Cargo Theft.")

11. **Employees should be restricted in the use of equipment designated "for company use only."** That might include photocopying machines, company gas pumps, telephones, and postage meters.

12. **Guests always should be escorted to their appointments by an employee.** That includes any visitor who is not a direct employee of the company.

13. **Security or management personnel should inspect or sift through rubbish piles or garbage containers,** looking for concealed items, at irregular intervals. If collusion between employees and trash collectors is suspected, rubbish in trucks should be inspected and security or management should supervise trash pickups. The pickup of trash from areas near valuable merchandise or materials should not be permitted.

14. **Employees should be assured that the identity of anyone who reports dishonesty on the part of other employees will be held in confidence.** Telephone hot lines can be installed or offers of rewards for such information posted, but management should keep in mind that many honest employees may be unwilling to inform on fellow workers and that the system can be misused to satisfy personal grudges.

15. **Management should adopt a tough, "zero-shortage" policy.** Even if you decide that a certain write-off due to pilferage is acceptable, keep that decision confidential and insist to employees that theft will not be tolerated.

Embezzlement

The embezzler's crime involves the fraudulent appropriation or conversion to personal use or benefit of company money or property. Culprits commonly are highly trusted employees who have access to a company's records, cash, and/or merchandise. Their crimes range from simple cash register thefts of small amounts of money to elaborate, long-term schemes involving the juggling of company books to conceal the theft of thousands or even millions of dollars in cash or merchandise.

The Small Business Administration reports embezzlers generally have been given more authority than was necessary in their positions. Also, fraud commonly occurs when companies neglect to maintain a strict separation of three critical responsibilities – transaction authorization, cash collections and payments, and record keeping.

The methods used by embezzlers are limited only by the imagination. The most common schemes – nonregistered sales, lapping, check kiting, payroll fraud, the creation of dummy suppliers, and expense account fraud – are briefly described below.

Nonregistered sales occur when a cashier purposely fails to ring a sale in the cash register and then steals the cash that should have been deposited for the sale. Most nonregistered sales are make possible by situations in which a customer pressed for time leaves the store without a receipt. The cashier may then ring an amount less than that received or make a "no sale" ring. Most cashiers who commit this crime keep secret records of the amount they have accumulated in the drawer so they can remove the correct amount of cash when the opportunity arises.

Lapping involves the temporary withholding of funds, such as payments on accounts receivable. This form of embezzlement is an ongoing scheme that usually starts with the theft of a small amount of cash but can run into thousands of dollars. For example, an employee responsible for recording payments to a company pockets a fifty-dollar cash payment. He then covers the theft by applying part of a separate, larger payment to the fifty-dollar invoice. The employee continues to skim funds from payments to cover previous short payments and pockets increasingly large sums as the scheme expands.

The lapping scheme requires the dishonest employee to keep close track of the various shortages and transfers to avoid drawing attention to a short account. The embezzler usually has access to accounts receivable records and can continually alter statements to customers so that this type of fraud may continue undetected for years.

Check kiting can be accomplished only by an employee who is in a position to write checks and make deposits in two or more bank accounts. One of these accounts will be a company account; the other is usually an account opened by the employee in his or her own name. Less often, both will be company accounts in different banks. And in yet another scenario, the second account will be with another company where an accomplice of the embezzler is working the same scheme on his employer.

The dishonest check writer takes advantage of the "float," or the period between when a company deposits a check and the bank collects the funds. Assuming a three-day "float," an embezzler can carry out the following check kiting scheme.

On day one a check for $5,000 drawn on Bank A is deposited in Bank B. The next day the check kiter cashes a check for $5,000, drawn on Bank B, with a teller at Bank B. Since the original kited check will be presented to Bank A for collection of funds on day four, the check kiter will deposit a check on or before that date in Bank A for $6,000 drawn on Bank B. This both ensures payment of the original kited check and increases the amount of the kite. As the process is repeated, the amounts of the kited checks become larger, more cash is withdrawn, and the scheme can continue until the shortage is uncovered – or until the kite string "breaks" when one of the banks refuses to honor a kited check because the funds on deposit are uncollected.

Payroll fraud occurs when a dishonest employee, usually one involved in payroll activities or a member of management with the authority to hire, adds the names of relatives or fictitious individuals to the company payroll. Payroll checks issued to those individuals are then either cashed by the relative and split with the employee or cashed by the employee under a falsified signature.

Dummy suppliers may be created by an employee who has the authority to conduct purchases on behalf of the company. The employee falsifies documentation to authorize a nonexistent purchase, "bills" the company for the purchase, and subsequently pays the fictitious invoice. In some cases, large corporations have paid thousands of dollars for purchases that were never actually made to companies that existed in name only.

Expense account fraud is one of the easiest and most common ways employees embezzle funds. Personal items may be bought and charged to the company, receipts may be falsified to document expense account claims, or expenses may be charged to the company for "entertaining" individuals who could not legitimately be considered current or potential customers. In a related offense, employees with liberal telephone accounts may charge to their employer numerous personal long-distance calls.

Read the signs. Embezzlers may tip their hands to the alert businessperson through some of these telltale signs:

- Accounting, inventory, and other company books that are not kept up to date.
- Customer invoices that habitually are mailed late.
- Frequent complaints by customers that statements are inaccurate.
- Employees who regularly turn down promotions or refuse vacations.
- Employees who frequently ask for cash advances on paychecks.
- Employees who frequently are entertained by suppliers or

who submit expense accounts that include costly entertainment charges.

- Employees whose standards of living are much higher than seems possible on their income.
- Frequent inventory shortages.
- Slow collections, which may indicate that payments are being sidetracked on their way to the company's bank account.
- Unusual bad-debt write-offs by the accounting department.

Theft prevention. The Small Business Administration (SBA) indicates that one of the most important steps the owner or manager of a business can take to prevent embezzlement is to set a positive and clear-cut example of the proper manner of conducting business. Employers who dip into petty cash, fudge on expense accounts, or use company funds or equipment for personal activities may unwittingly encourage employees to follow their lead.

An employer should establish and maintain a working climate of accountability in which accurate records are kept and regularly audited. The following precautions also can help to cut down on the possibility of embezzlement:

1. **Carefully check the background of prospective employees,** particularly those to be given fiduciary responsibilities. This check should include oral and written contacts with previous employers, credit bureaus, and personal references. Make sure that an employee who will handle funds is adequately bonded.

2. **An owner or member of senior management should supervise the accounting employee** who opens and records receipts of checks, cash payments, and money orders.

3. **Bank deposits should be prepared daily and made by an owner or manager.** Duplicate deposit slips, stamped "received" by the bank, should always be returned to the accounting department.The reconciliation of bank statements and canceled checks should be done by an employee who does not draw or sign checks. Management should examine canceled checks and endorsements for unusual features. (Also see Chapter 12, "Check Fraud.")

4. **All payments should be approved by senior management as well as by the person who draws or signs the checks.** Senior management should examine all invoices and supporting data before signing checks. Management should verify that merchandise was received and that prices seem reasonable. In many false purchase schemes, the embezzler will neglect to make up receiving forms or other records purporting to show receipt of merchandise.

5. **All paid invoices should be marked "canceled" and filed in a secure area to prevent double payment.** Dishonest accounting department employees have been known to make out and receive approval on duplicate checks for the same invoice. The second check may be embezzled by the employee or by an accomplice at the company issuing the invoice.

6. **Prenumbered checkbooks and other prenumbered forms should be periodically inspected** to ensure that checks or forms from the back or middle of the book have not been removed for use in a fraudulent scheme.

7. **Salespeople should not be permitted to process transactions affecting their own accounts.** The same rule applies to employees responsible for assigning projects to outside suppliers.

8. **Names placed on payroll should be authorized in writing by a specifically designated company official.** Payroll should be prepared by one person, checked by another, and distributed by others not involved with payroll preparation or time slip approvals.

9. **Shipments should be authorized and accounted for by an employee who is not also responsible for controlling inventories.** An employee who maintains inventory records should not participate in physical counts of inventory or in reconciliation of physical counts with the records.

10. **Where nonregistered sales are suspected, retail establishments may effectively enlist the customer's assistance.** Signs posted by each cash register announcing that any customer who does not receive a sales receipt with every purchase is entitled to a cash bonus may help to put an end to the problem. Also effective are outside

"shoppers," who may be hired through private shopping services and, sometimes, local women's clubs or auxiliaries. Shoppers are provided with funds to make purchases in the store – they can provide valuable information on whether sales are being recorded properly, and on the proficiency and courtesy of salespeople. Another, more expensive deterrent is a new, high-tech antitheft system being used by some retailers to keep a closer eye on employees. The closed circuit surveillance system allows managers to view cashiers on one side of a split screen videomonitor and cash register receipts on the other.

11. **Customer complaints should be received and investigated by a company official who is not on the accounting department staff.**

WHAT TO DO IF YOU ARE VICTIMIZED

Vigorously prosecuting suspected *pilferers* can be one of the most effective deterrents to further theft. However, the SBA cautions that business managers who suspect an employee is stealing goods or commodities should not attempt to solve the crime themselves. Instead, contact your local police department or a reliable professional security consultant.

If you believe your company has been the victim of an embezzlement scheme, it is important not to *confront the suspect.* All too often, situations that seem to indicate impropriety on the part of an employee turn out to have perfectly valid explanations. The SBA reports cases in which employees have been charged with embezzlement, dismissed from their positions, and later found to be entirely innocent. A false accusation could involve your company in a lawsuit.

If you suspect an employee is embezzling company funds, contact a trustworthy independent accountant who can thoroughly examine company books. If, with the guidance of your accountant, you still believe that one or more employees may be guilty of embezzlement, contact your attorney for advice on how to proceed. Discuss with your attorney the necessity of notifying the bonding company and appropriate law enforcement authorities. It is particularly important to follow legal advice in matters regarding prosecution in order to avoid charges of false arrest.

CHAPTER 17

Bribery, Kickbacks, and Payoffs

THE CASE OF
The Collusive Consultant

The head of research at one major corporation is responsible for "farming out" special projects to qualified consultants and subcontractors. A subcontractor bidding on a large project invites her to discuss business over lunch. The research head mentions that money has been tight and raises small at her company in recent years. She is hoping to supplement her income by doing some outside consulting. Independent consultants are often used by his firm, says the subcontractor. If he is awarded this particular job, his firm could probably use the services of someone with her professional expertise.

At subsequent meetings the research head and subcontractor become more at ease in discussing the arrangement. They agree on a "mutually beneficial" plan – she will provide outside professional advice for a monthly fee of $1,000; the silent arrangement will run the length of the contract.

The subcontractor is recommended for the project and approved. Work runs several months longer than expected but is completed satisfactorily, according to the report submitted by the research head to her superiors. Subsequent projects are bid on and awarded to the same subcontractor.

Over the following ten years, the research head receives more than $100,000 in "consultant fees" from the subcontractor. These fees are passed along in the subcontractor's bills – which are approved by the head of research.

Behind the Schemes

Arrangements such as the one described above involve employees and public and private officials at virtually every level of government, industry, business, and labor. The motivating factors behind bribery, kickback, and payoff schemes are innumerable. Most common among the goals of perpetrators are attempts to:

- Obtain new business or retain old business.
- Solicit approval on plans or permits from government officials.
- Influence local, state, or federal legislation.
- Obtain government licenses.
- Obtain approval on loans.
- Prevent work stoppages due to actions of union officials.
- Obtain proprietary information.
- Obtain approvals on falsified financial statements.
- Encourage the sale of stocks or bonds at distorted prices.
- Obtain information on bids submitted by contractors.
- Facilitate the sale of inferior products or services.
- Sway the minds of law enforcement officials.
- Pay off gambling or other personal debts.
- Cover up the lavish use of entertainment or other company funds.

Two Types of Schemes

While variations on these schemes run into the thousands, the majority can be grouped into two categories: schemes involving dealings between business and government, and schemes involving dealings among private-sector parties.

Research by the federal government's National Advisory Commission on Criminal Justice Standards and Goals as well as the U.S. Chamber of Commerce led to the development of a series of questions that should be asked when bribery, kickback, or payoff schemes are suspected. Affirmative answers to any of the following questions do not necessarily indicate fraudulent activity but should be regarded as signs that something could be awry.

In Government-Business Dealings

1. Do respected and well-qualified companies refuse to conduct business with the city, state, or federal agency?

2. Are government contracts awarded to a small number of firms?

3. Is competitive bidding not required?

4. Are there frequent "emergency" situations that do not require competitive bidding?

5. Are professional services bid "by invitation only"?

6. Have low bids been disclosed and the low-bidding companies subsequently disqualified for unspecified technical reasons?

7. Do businesses encounter significant delays when applying for county, local, state, or federal licenses, such as liquor licenses and building permits?

8. Are government procedures so complicated that a go-between is often required to unravel the mystery and get through to the right people?

9. Do government officials or employees have financial or other interests in businesses competing for government business?

10. Have public officials accepted high posts with companies to which their agencies have recently awarded contracts?

11. Are antibribery statutes ineffective or limited in scope to cover department heads only?

12. Do large campaign contributions precede (or follow) favorable government rulings?

13. Are costs of conducting similar business operations, after allowances are made for legitimate differences in labor rates, transportation, and other factors, markedly different in two counties or states?

In Business-to-Business Dealings

1. Are reputable dealers uninterested in submitting bids?

2. Is there frequent use, without periodic bidding, of the same supplier?

3. Do certain employees pass up opportunities for promotion for questionable reasons?

4. Does an employee frequently socialize with a supplier?

5. Is the standard of living of anyone who influences company purchases higher than can be explained by wage or salary levels or other legitimate sources of income?

6. Does the cost of certain goods or services seem inexplicably high?

7. Does one individual hold the sole responsibility for calling for, reviewing, and approving bids?

8. Are there vague "extra charges"?

9. Does an employee who influences the selection of suppliers have a financial interest in, or relatives employed by, current suppliers?

10. Does an employee who influences the selection of suppliers obtain tickets for sporting events, concerts, or other social galas with inexplicable ease?

HOW TO PROTECT YOUR BUSINESS

Both the National Advisory Commission on Criminal Justice Standards and Goals and the U.S. Chamber of Commerce recommend these measures to combat bribery, payoff, and kickback schemes:

In Government-Business Dealings

1. Management in both government and business should prohibit the exchange of gifts, regardless of value.

2. Government and business should ban all activities that carry even the appearance of impropriety.

3. Local and state governments should appoint and maintain nonpolitical commissions to continually monitor and investigate possible official corruption.

4. Solicitations of payoffs by public officials should be reported to appropriate law enforcement agencies.

In Business-to-Business Dealings

1. Businesses should separate receiving from purchasing operations so buyers cannot accept short deliveries in return for kickbacks.

2. Businesses should require competitive bidding.

3. An executive from outside the purchasing department should review bids and inspect incoming goods.

4. Employees, particularly those in purchasing, should be required to file monthly reports on gifts and gratuities received. A limit should be set on the value of gifts that may be accepted.

5. Management should insist that gifts come to the office, not to employees' homes.

6. Vendors should be informed of acceptable gift giving practices.

7. Businesses should insist that, in cases when a supplier other than the low bidder is selected, the reason be documented and sent to top management for review and approval.

8. Purchasing agents and suppliers should be rotated periodically.

9. Employees should be instructed to report any demands by customers for payoffs.

10. Estimates of reasonable costs for products and services should be developed so that possible kickback costs can be identified.

11. Policies should be developed that ensure maintenance of a professional distance between management and union officials.

12. Procedures should be instituted that alert management when payments of "commissions" are not documented by the usual paperwork, when "commissions" are not in line with recognized trade practices, and when payments are made through banks not usually used.

WHAT TO DO IF YOU ARE VICTIMIZED

An employee or official of a company or government organization involved in a bribery, kickback, or payoff scheme may have violated any of a number of local, state, or federal laws.

If you suspect that one of your employees is either receiving or giving bribes or kickbacks in dealings with another non-government firm, *do not confront the suspect immediately.* Instead, discuss your suspicions with your company attorney to determine what action and investigation can be undertaken and what laws apply. It is essential that your business stay within the letter of the law; therefore, do not attempt an investigation on your own. And remember, it is not necessary that a bribe, kickback, or payoff actually be received in order for a crime to have been committed. Under most existing legislation, the mere offering, conferring, or agreeing to confer a benefit is considered an offense.

CHAPTER 18

Insurance Fraud

THE CASE OF
The Crooked Claimant

A corporation provides automobiles for use by employees on company business, but occasionally a car is difficult to come by and employees are called upon to use their own vehicles. In these instances, the company provides mileage and usage reimbursement and accident coverage under a rider to its vehicle insurance policy.

One salesperson, who often goes directly from his home to client locations, reports early on a Monday morning that his car has been the victim of a hit-and-run accident. He is instructed to summon local police to the parking lot where the accident occurred. The police subsequently file an accident report and the company's insurance policy covers the repairs to the employee's car, less the $200 deductible, which is paid by the company.

The company is unaware that the car actually was damaged in a single-car accident over the weekend. Rather than contact his own insurance company and pay the deductible, plus risk the possibility of an increase in his insurance rates, the employee waited until Monday, drove to a client's office, and then reported the accident for filing at his employer's expense.

Common Types of Insurance Fraud

The American Insurance Association, representing more than 250 major insurance companies, estimates that anywhere from 10 to 25 percent of all claims filed may be fraudulent. The estimate's wide range, says an AIA spokesperson, results from the number of possible interpretations of the term "insurance fraud," with the 10 percent figure limited to such highly fraudulent activities as auto theft rings and organized crime activities and the 25 percent figure including even "small" frauds, such as claim figures submitted that are higher than actual costs.

A 1991 American Insurance Association estimate put total annual losses due to fraud at $20 billion, a dramatic increase from a 1974 estimate of $1.5 billion. And even this $20 billion figure is a conservative estimate, reflecting only direct, accountable losses.

Nondirect losses due to insurance fraud include the increase built into insurance policy premiums to cover fraudulent claims. Those fraudulent claims account for an average of one dollar out of every ten dollars paid by insurance companies in claims. Other unaccounted-for losses to business include the lost services of employees "recuperating" from fake accidents or illnesses and unwarranted out-of-court settlements paid to insurance con artists by businesses wishing to avoid costly legal proceedings.

Because many businesspeople look upon insurance coverage as an unavoidable cost of doing business, they may not spend enough time examining how their policies work, what is and is not insured, and how insurance fraud can harm their business. Although a full treatment of the subject of insurance demands its own book, the most common types of insurance fraud are generally quite simple to understand. These schemes include:

- The creation of fictitious insurance companies that exist only in their paper policies.

- The sale of policies by insurance companies that do not adhere to widely accepted business and insurance industry standards and as a result are more susceptible to failure and bankruptcy.

- The oversale of insurance, resulting in coverage more extensive than is necessary.

- The fraudulent and deceitful activities of customers and employees that result in unwarranted insurance claims.

- The withholding of information by insurance agents that businesses need to shop for competitive medical insurance rates.

HOW TO PROTECT YOUR BUSINESS

Avoid "Paper Firms"

To avoid doing business with a fictitious insurance company, your business should make a thorough investigation of the company being considered. Contact your local Better Business Bureau (see Appendix B) and the area office of your state insurance commissioner, listed in your telephone directory, for a report on the company. Request a copy of the firm's financial statement and have your accountant review the document to confirm that it has been certified by a reputable accounting firm and that the members of the company's board are reputable and serve in the company's best interest.

Do not hesitate to ask the insurance company for bank and business client references and to contact those references. Ask business clients for details of their associations with the insurance company – has it been responsive to their requests, made an effort to keep policies up-to-date, and kept them abreast of changes in the insurance industry that may affect their business?

Be particularly painstaking in your investigations when considering doing business with a foreign insurance firm.

Watch Out for Unsound Business Practices

To avoid doing business with an insurance company that fails to adhere to accepted industry standards, observe the precautions detailed above, paying particular attention to the state insurance commissioner's advice. Where little information is available about the financial stability of an insurance company, as may be the case with a firm located outside the U.S., ask a trusted business investment counselor, such as a banker or broker, to assist in determining the insurer's stability and reliability. If doubts remain, look for another company.

Monitor the Amount of Coverage

There is a fine line between the proper amount of insurance coverage and too little or too much coverage. While it is important for a business to build a close working relationship with a reliable and responsive insurance broker, it also makes sense occasionally to have a competitive firm review your coverage with an eye to potential loopholes or excesses.

A colleague in a similar business, or a trade or business association to which you belong may be able to provide you with recommendations on business insurance coverage and the reliability of various insurers. Some associations offer group insurance packages as part of their member services. These packages may offer competitive rates and, because the insurer is familiar with the particular business, may have a better understanding of needs unique to the association's members.

As a result of recent industry and legislative actions, insurance policies have become more understandable to the layperson. Take the time to read and understand the policy you are investing in, address questions to the insurer, and insist on satisfactory answers. If you are concerned about the adequacy of a policy, consult your attorney or a legal firm specializing in insurance claims. Most insurance brokers, like any professional salesperson, will attempt to sell you the most comprehensive, and often the most expensive, policy. Legal counsel specializing in insurance coverage should be able to help to pare away any unnecessary coverage.

Examine All Claims for Potential Fraud

Perhaps the most effective way to reduce insurance losses due to employee or customer dishonesty is through a meticulous, knowledgeable examination of claims and potential fraud. Management should be on the alert for chronically ill employees who regularly file insurance or disability claims on the company policy, and should insist on the option of calling for a second medical opinion by a physician of the company's choice. Management and employees should also be alerted to the scam practiced by damage claim artists, who feign injury while on company property, threaten to sue, and then offer to accept an out-of-court settlement. Whenever possible, injured customers should be directed to a company or company-retained physician for examination. When customers or employees claim damage to personal property, local police and an attorney representing the company should be contacted immediately.

A report by the U.S. Chamber of Commerce lists the following "tip-offs" for false insurance claims:

- The person who fell or suffered an accident expresses a desire for an expeditious settlement.

- The claimant seems to have used exceptional dispatch in retaining an attorney.

- The claimant appears extraordinarily knowledgeable about the terminology and workings of the claim adjustment process.

- An injured claimant is treated at a hospital operated by his personal physician.

- The claimant's physician, despite repeated requests, fails to itemize bills.

- Several injured parties are all treated by the same physician.

- The claimant uses a lawyer-physician combination that has been implicated in prior suspected frauds.

- Attempts to contact an employee claiming lost time due to an injury go unanswered.

Be Alert to Medical Insurance Scams

The United States spends more on medical services than any other country, and over the past decade the cost of those services has skyrocketed. Between 1979 and 1989, health care costs increased 119 percent, to an alarming 11.4 percent of this country's gross national product. It's not surprising that medical insurance costs are one of the five most expensive items for most businesses today. In fact, those costs equal, by one estimate, more than half of pretax profits for the average company.

Businesses have responded to soaring medical insurance premiums in a variety of ways: by introducing alternative health care plans, such as health maintenance organizations (HMOs) and preferred provider organizations (PPOs); requiring higher deductibles, caps on the employee's share of premiums, and cost sharing, or copayment of plans previously funded entirely

Insurance Companies Fight Back

Insurance companies pay out billions of dollars each year in settlement for fraudulent claims that include staged accidents, phony burglaries, padded doctors' bills, falsified product liability claims, and one of the largest and most dangerous schemes, arson for profit. In 1990, there were an estimated ninety-seven thousand structural fires of suspicious or incendiary origin, which resulted in 715 civilian deaths and $1.394 billion in property damage, according to the National Fire Protection Association.

Insurance cheats come from all walks of life. Organized crime groups, terrorist organizations that stage accidents and file claims as a means of raising funds, unscrupulous professionals, including doctors, lawyers, and chiropractors, and otherwise honest consumers who do not regard insurance fraud as a "serious" crime have been found to participate.

To combat insurance fraud, several states have created special fraud investigation bureaus within the states' insurance departments. Computerized fraud detection systems have proven highly successful in cracking fraud cases. And, increasingly, insurance companies are setting up special units of their own to investigate suspect claims.

The dilemma faced by every insurance company, says the National Association of Independent Insurers, is how to identify claims warranting an intensive investigation before settlement. Special investigative units staffed by fraud specialists, working with a company's claims department, are helping to solve that problem. While insurance industry experts note that insurance fraud probably cannot be prevented, most agree that special antifraud units can save insurance companies millions of dollars – costs that otherwise would be passed on to businesses and consumers.

by employers; and instituting rewards and penalties for life-style choices, such as smoking or weight control, that affect their employees' health.

Any of these approaches may prove effective in controlling your company's medical insurance costs. You also should be aware, however, that in an era of rising costs and shrinking revenues, some insurance companies may resort to unethical practices to retain your business. Those practices can cost you money. Here's a look at a few of the tactics commonly used:

☐ **Withholding information.** In order to shop around for competitive quotes on medical insurance coverage, a business needs detailed information on its past history, such as a

Property Damaged by Arson in 1989		
Property Classification	**Number of Offenses**	**Average Monetary Value of Damage**
STRUCTURES: TOTAL	43,672	$21,410
Single Occupancy Residential	19,220	14,364
Other Residential	8,034	13,337
Storage	4,326	27,123
Industrial/ Manufacturing	682	113,778
Other Commercial	4,949	45,672
Community/Public	4,008	16,652
Other Structures	2,453	26,128
MOBILE VEHICLES: TOTAL	21,631	4,902
Motor Vehicles	19,962	4,636
Other Mobile Vehicles	1,669	8,078
OTHER: TOTAL	15,277	835
TOTAL	**80,580**	**13,078**

Source: *Crime in the United States*, 1989
U.S. Department of Justice
Federal Bureau of Investigation

description of past claims and the loss ratio of paid claims to premiums. An insurance agent determined to hold onto your business – and his or her commission – may stall in providing that information until you are forced to renew your existing policy or accept the agent's alternative in order to avoid interrupting your coverage.

☐ **Rising rates.** In a related ruse, the agent may delay in notifying you of premium changes until shortly before they take effect, again preventing you from seeking competitive quotes.

☐ **Possessive agents.** Some insurance carriers refuse to release a company's historic claims information to anyone but the company's current agent. This makes it easier for the agent to carry out the two schemes described above.

☐ **Possessive carriers.** Some insurance carriers refuse to release historic claims information *at all,* particularly to companies with a small number of employees. Although this practice is illegal in some states, in others carriers are within their rights to withhold the information.

If your insurance agent delays in providing needed loss information, your recourses include going over the agent's head directly to the insurance carrier for the information or securing a new agent. In most cases, to transfer your account to a more cooperative agent, you need only direct the carrier to reassign you to a specified agency or to another agent within the same agency. If your agent or carrier still prove uncooperative, you may contact your state insurance commissioner, listed in your phone directory, for advice and assistance.

WHAT TO DO IF YOU ARE VICTIMIZED

Alleged false insurance claims by customers or employees and illegal practices by representatives or insurance companies should be brought to the immediate attention of your company attorney and or state insurance commissioner. Your attorney may advise you to contact local police, to refuse to honor an insurance claim, or to file a countersuit in court. In any case, since the recourse to insurance fraud almost always involves legal action, your response should be entrusted to a competent legal professional.

CHAPTER 19

Computer Crime

 THE CASE OF
The Systematic Stickup

The owner of an investment firm believes that all company records and management functions have been successfully transferred to a highly efficient, cost-effective, in-house computer system. The transformation required hiring computer consultants who proved invaluable in setting up and explaining the new system of management and information storage and retrieval. For more than a year, the system appeared to be working almost flawlessly. But now, occasional discrepancies are showing up between the computer's financial printouts and the statements provided by the company's bank.

A thorough review of the computer's records and programming activities uncovers the culprit. Apparently, the computer consultant took advantage of his full access to the computer and its confidential contents to hide several lines of undocumented computer code in a program instructing the computer to disburse funds to a company that supposedly works for the investment firm. In reality, the funds are sent by the computer to a bank account opened under the consultant's name. Other codes alter financial records within the computer to camouflage the activities, circumventing built-in system safeguards. The conniving consultant also prudently entered undocumented codes that, when he accesses the computer over the phone lines, instructs it to issue an electronic warning if the system has been tampered with. Consequently, before the consultant can be sought for questioning, he has cleared his bank account of some $150,000 in fraudulently obtained funds and disappeared.

Computer Vulnerability: Easy Access to Business Data

Computers have moved into the workplace at a speed virtually unprecedented by any other piece of business equipment. Not even the telephone, which in its advent revolutionized business communications, has had so pervasive an impact on how business is conducted and managed.

Every day, hundreds of companies turn over many of the details of their management functions and controls to these high-tech tools. In 1989, the U.S. Census Bureau reported 36.8 percent of the population, or some 40 million Americans used a computer at work – a 50 percent increase over the 1984 figure.

Few successes come without their price, and while these dramatic advancements may improve significantly the quality and cost-effectiveness of a company's services to clients, employees, and stockholders, they also lead to unprecedented opportunities for crime. Computers are inherently vulnerable. Employees must have access to their company's computers – restricting that access can make developing a product or providing a service more difficult, encumbering the very features that make the computer so valuable. Yet easy access creates ample opportunities for fraud. Thieves can transfer proprietary information from a mainframe to a small floppy disk, which can easily be concealed and taken from the premises. Competitors can invade the system over the phone lines or through the use of readily available and relatively inexpensive electronic equipment. Trusted employees can alter computer records to embezzle funds. Vindictive ex-employees can introduce computer "viruses" – secret programs designed to alter or destroy the data on hard or floppy disks.

Estimates of the cost of computer crime to U.S. businesses vary, largely because most companies choose not to risk the publicity that follows reports of security breaches. Various sources put the toll at between three billion and five billion dollars annually. That includes an estimated five hundred million dollars in losses to the telecommunications industry from the illegal use of telephone access codes and about one hundred million dollars in illicit electronic fund transfers. Experts predict that those figures will soar as a generation reared on computers comes of age and computer crime becomes increasingly sophisticated. At the same time, federal officials warn that criminals needn't be computer experts to ply their trade. In fact, a recent study by the U.S. General Accounting Office disclosed that most computer-related crimes today are committed by individuals with a limited knowledge of computer technology. Further, not all computer crime requires sophisticated equipment. An amateur computer enthusiast, or "hacker," equipped only with an inexpensive personal computer, a TV monitor, and a modem – a device that enables computer signals to be transmitted over telephone lines – can easily gain access to an unprotected computer network by phone and, intentionally or unwittingly, probe, alter, and even destroy some or all of the files in the computer's memory.

Typical Computer Crimes

Most computer crimes fall into one of five categories, each category named for the primary area of crime. Following are brief descriptions of crimes in the areas of programming activities, computer time, input data, output data, and data transfer.

1. **Programming crimes.** A computer programmer enters instructions directing the computer to manipulate data in a specific way. Such cases have included:

   - A computer science student who injected a virus into a Defense Department data network, disrupting military, university, and corporate research computers across the nation.

   - A discharged insurance broker who planted a "time bomb" in his employer's computer: a program designed to activate two days after he left the job, destroying thousands of employee records and holding up payroll checks for weeks.

   - Another postdated programming instruction that directed a company's computer to transfer funds to an account opened by a former employee.

   - A programmer who so enjoyed travel that she built timed malfunctions into programs owned by clients around the U.S. This way she could plan on making frequent "working trips" to various parts of the country.

The outright theft of programs also has become commonplace. At a time when copyrighted programs can cost thousands of dollars, determined hobbyists and software pirates are breaking through security codes to copy programs for personal use or sale. Dishonest employees, customers, and others with access to computer facilities may simply walk off with unguarded floppy disks that contain backup or original programs.

2. **Misuse of computer time.** Whether it involves playing games on a company-owned computer or operating a personal business using an employer's facilities, the unauthorized use of businesses' computer facilities is one of the most costly and pervasive computer crimes.

   Much of this misuse takes place during nonpeak periods, such as lunch breaks and after business hours. While this type of crime is similar to the misuse of a company's photocopier or office supplies, it can be far costlier and much harder to trace. In at least one known case, a business actually purchased a larger, more sophisticated computer system to accommodate what it assumed was a rapidly expanding business workload. In fact, the workload was expanding due to increased personal use of the easily accessible facilities.

3. **Manipulation of input data.** According to the U.S. General Accounting Office, most computer-related crime results from the preparation of false input data to computer-based systems. Crimes involving input data encompass all deceptive activities that manipulate, withhold, or fabricate data placed in the computer's memory for later use. Perhaps the simplest of these cons involves the withholding or outright destruction of information to cover pilferage or embezzlement. For example, lists of a company's inventory may be destroyed, leaving the computer and, in turn, management in the dark when it comes to tracing inventory flow. This can allow the thief time to make off with a great deal of merchandise before inventory can be reviewed.

   Tampering with data can include the addition of names of fictitious suppliers to lists of approved vendors. Subsequent instructions might authorize payments ostensibly made to the nonexistent suppliers that actually find their way into the programmer's pockets.

4. **Theft of computer output.** Perhaps the easiest and most directly damaging form of computer crime involves the theft of computer output. The thief simply steals what the computer produces, including printouts or punch cards of mailing lists or customer lists and other confidential information.

There have been numerous cases of employees using stolen customer lists to start their own competitive businesses or selling lists of current customer orders to competitive firms. Industrial theft also includes cases of computer espionage. For example, an eavesdropper a mile away from a company's facilities, armed with relatively inexpensive electronic equipment, can tap into the display on its competitor's computer screens or the data being printed out on its computer printers. These computer tappers gain easy, unobserved access to client lists, financial information, passwords, and other proprietary data.

5. **Theft by data transfer.** One of the true miracles of the computer revolution has been the ability it confers of transporting virtual libraries of information over telephone lines in minutes or even seconds. Unfortunately, this miraculous capability also presents one of the weakest links in computer security.

Data transfer over telephone lines normally takes place between a video display terminal and the company computer it is connected to, or between two separate computers exchanging information via a modem. Confidential information being transferred between two points can be intercepted by means of direct wiretaps, electromagnetic sensing devices that record radiation generated by the computer's central processor, or illegal entries into the information network. Illegal entries are accomplished when unauthorized terminals intercept signals transmitted by authorized terminals. The unauthorized terminal then instructs the computer network to remain open and allow the unauthorized user access to its contents. For this breach of security to take place, the system must be equipped with a telephone hookup that enables the hacker to gain entry. Thus, this type of system is particularly vulnerable to outside threats.

Desktop Forgery

Counterfeiters have discovered a new tool: the personal computer. Using the technology of desktop publishing, which allows businesses to prepare professional-looking documents on inexpensive personal computers, desktop forgers are able to duplicate almost any kind of official document.

The U.S. Secret Service uncovered its first case of computer forgery in 1989, and experts fear that, once forgers become familiar with desktop technology, this type of fraud will mushroom. Using relatively inexpensive and widely available equipment – typically a personal computer, a desktop publishing program, and a laser printer – a forger can cheaply and easily duplicate passports, birth certificates, stock certificates, purchase orders, cash and credit card receipts, bank checks, and a wide range of other papers, all bearing the official logos or emblems of the original documents. Bills can be paid with bogus checks, shoplifters can offer forged receipts when returning stolen merchandise for refund, and con artists can use forged identification to open credit, charge card, or bank accounts.

Your business can help to foil the desktop forger by:

- **Using difficult-to-replicate emblems or other devices on company documents**. You may not discourage the most dedicated thief but you might make his less determined counterpart look elsewhere for a victim.

- **Using color on important documents.** A new generation of color copiers that print on ordinary paper are making the forger's job easier, but it is still harder to reproduce color than black and white.

- **Ordering nonstandard paper for your printing needs.** Anticounterfeiting aids include specially treated paper that displays the word "VOID" when tampered with.

Recent cases of data transfer theft have included:

- A discharged employee of a software maker who used her telephone to gain entry into her former employer's system and copy millions of dollars' worth of company products.

- A ring of computer crooks who tapped into phone lines transmitting bank account transactions to a network of shared automatic teller machines (ATMs). The thieves then encoded bank customers' personal ATM code numbers on magnetic strips to create bogus ATM cards.

HOW TO PROTECT YOUR BUSINESS

A variety of security measures are available to help a business safeguard its computer system. Some restrict access to the company computer, increasing security but requiring management to weigh the cost of theft losses against possible decreases in efficiency, productivity, and morale. Some security measures are expensive, again requiring a consideration of the relative costs of crime and prevention. Following is an overview of security procedures and devices. Some of these may prove useful in your company's efforts to increase security while maintaining a productive work environment.

- **Implementation.** Decisions about implementing a security system should be made *before* the system is installed. Experience has shown that during transition periods – those weeks or months during which a company transfers its manual systems of record keeping to a computer system – businesses are the most susceptible to computer crime. Therefore, crime watchers recommend that a well-planned, clear-cut security system be implemented from day one. As an added precaution during the transition period, companies are encouraged to continue their manual system of record keeping in addition to the computer's record keeping. This overlapping should continue for at least two months or for as long as it takes to remove the major "bugs" from the new system.

- **Employee hiring.** Thorough background checks on individuals being considered for key computer positions should include direct contacts with former employers, professional and personal references, verification of technical skills, and credit checks. The greatest threat to a company's secrets often is a lack of employee awareness and concern about computer security. To combat this problem, a company relying on the security of its computer system should develop a clearly written security policy and periodically remind and instruct employees in security procedures. In addition, new employees should be asked to sign a confidentiality agreement spelling out the company's policy on proper use of the computer and its definition of proprietary data. A confidentiality agreement makes employees liable for their actions. For the document to be legally viable, however, employers must make certain that it conforms to federal and state privacy laws as well as to current company personnel guidelines, employment policies, and union contracts. It is also critical that the employee have sufficient opportunity to read and review the agreement before signing and that he or she enter into the agreement voluntarily.

- **Access to computer facilities.** Only those employees whose work requires that they have access to computer facilities should be allowed in the computer area. Identities of repair personnel and technicians from outside the company should be verified by asking for identification and calling the company they represent. Also confirm that a service call was placed by someone with the authority to do so. A company employee should accompany the technician to the worksite, and a log book should be maintained with the names and times of all who have access to the computer facilities.

- **Physical security.** To ensure security, computer facilities should be located in relatively low traffic areas. Ideally, equipment should be located in an isolated area containing adequate lighting, few windows or doors, and a securely locking entrance. Security experts recommend that companies concerned about the threat of industrial espionage group their computers together – the radiation emitted by computers thus combines to make a babble that is hard for electromagnetic eavesdropping equipment to read. Placing computer facilities in the middle of the building also helps to foil eavesdroppers, thanks to the interference created by the building's telephone lines, structural steel, and other elements. Ideally, a security guard should be posted at each entrance to the computer facilities. Guards should be required to check the identification of everyone requesting access. Some companies provide employees with photo identification cards, others with cards containing fingerprints and/or codes that can be verified only by a deciphering machine at the computer facilities entrance.

- **Functions and authority.** The computer processing department should be located physically apart from other departments. Employee functions and authority also should be separate, and no single employee should have control over an entire operation. The assignments of employees working in computer areas should be rotated on a regular basis.

- **Protective devices.** The company that sells or leases your computer equipment can explain how passwords, security codes, and code scrambling devices can help to control access to the system. The passwords you select should not be words or figures with a special significance, such as personal names or social security numbers. Passwords should be changed periodically, and employees should be instructed on proper procedures for keeping them confidential. Computers can be programmed in a variety of ways to thwart would-be interlopers – by "stalling" after each wrong password entry, disconnecting after a specified number of wrong guesses, recording penetration attempts, and even tracing a phone call after a certain number of unsuccessful phone attempts have been made.

  A wealth of other security devices can be built into or added onto a computer system. A qualified computer systems security consultant can help you select the security measures suited to your needs and budget. Current technology makes possible the use of:

  □ **Encryption systems,** which encode messages sent through the network, thus preventing unauthorized access. Some software publishers use encryption in the form of a "digital signature" tacked onto a program – the customer uses a paired device to verify the encoded signature and make certain no one has tampered with the program.

☐ **"Trusted systems,"** which make certain that employees can access only those files that are relevant to their job and perform only the functions they are authorized to perform.

☐ **Protective devices**, such as those used by U.S. intelligence agencies and some large corporations, that silence the electromagnetic noise emitted by computers and computer peripherals, thus preventing electromagnetic computer eavesdropping.

☐ **Security software** that uses passwords to control access to information contained in a hard disk.

☐ **Antivirus devices** designed to combat computer viruses – those potentially deadly coded instructions hidden in a computer program by a prankster or vindictive hacker that enable the program to modify or destroy data. Security devices include plug-in circuit boards that check for viruses and software programs that continually check for the presence of "alien" programs and sound an alert when a virus is spotted; other software programs are written specifically to recognize and eradicate common viruses. New computer viruses and new antivirus programs are constantly being developed. Check with your security consultant or local software dealer for current information. Experts also recommend these precautions to help stop the spread of computer viruses:

- Prohibit employees from exchanging computer programs and disks.

- Stop or limit the use of public domain and shareware programs.

- Prohibit the copying of pirated programs and programs from computer bulletin boards.

- Frequently copy files onto backup disks.

- Be cautious of software of unknown origin.

• **Storage procedures.** Programming materials and input and output data are only as safe as the storage system that contains them. Printout bins, disk files, and tape libraries should be kept in an orderly fashion in an untrafficked area set aside solely for storage purposes. These areas, like all other computer areas, should be protected from water leakage and temperature variances. Ideally, there should be no windows and no more than two access doors in the storage area.

Each document should be given a file number, which is recorded in a secure filing system, access to which is permitted only by written authorization from a specified member of management. The authorization should specify which documents are to be logged out and for what period of time, and documents removed from the storage area should be signed for on a carefully maintained daily register at the area's entrance.

Sensitive data should not be stored on easily accessed hard disks. Instead, you might transfer the data to floppy disks and maintain tight security over their storage, or use a portable storage device that can be kept in a locked drawer or other secure area. The disposal of computer materials also should be treated with caution, with paper shredders or burning devices used to keep discarded information from falling into the wrong hands.

- **Periodic audits.** Both internal and independent audits of a company's records and security systems should be conducted at least once a year. This is especially crucial during the start-up phase of internal computer management.

  The auditors should have considerable experience in computer analysis and programming as well as in accounting practices. Auditors may be expected to closely scrutinize a company's record keeping systems; some will attempt to defraud the company's system to test whether security is sufficient.

WHAT TO DO IF YOU ARE VICTIMIZED

When a computer crime is committed, the odds tend to favor the criminal. Industry's reluctance to report computer-related offenses and risk the resulting publicity contribute to a low rate of arrests and convictions. If a crime is detected and reported, local police departments often do not have the expertise to protect and retrieve electronically stored information that could be used as evidence. Police departments also may be unable to undertake the unusually time-consuming, complex, multijurisdictional investigations required in computer fraud. Further, most prosecutors are not computer experts and may not have the training to pursue electronic thieves. And even when computer criminals are successfully prosecuted, these white-collar criminals typically have received relatively light sentences.

There are signs that this dismal picture may be changing. Special investigative units have been set up in some police departments across the U.S., and several regions have established computer crime-fighting networks pooling the resources of police departments, prosecutors, courts, parole agencies, and other law enforcement entities. The federal agencies primarily involved in computer crime investigation – the FBI, Secret Service, and IRS – are training agents in the investigation of high-tech crimes. Major computer crime crackdowns conducted in 1990 included the cooperative activities of agents of the Department of Justice, FBI, and Secret Service as well as state and local authorities. Further, computer crime laws have been enacted in a number of states. A series of federal laws, including a landmark 1986 federal computer law, make it illegal for anyone to knowingly and without authorization access a computer in order to obtain information protected by other laws or executive orders, to alter or damage federal-interest computers, to commit a fraud, or to obtain or alter an electronic communication service's information if the violator is not a subscriber.

Your company's most effective recourse to computer crime begins with a willingness to investigate any and all questionable activities. Management should be constantly on the alert for indications of possible wrongdoing. Confidential information somehow turns up in an area where it doesn't belong or comes up in conversation between people who shouldn't have access to it; computer-generated data is found to be inconsistent with other business records; employees, customers, or suppliers complain about inaccurate computer-generated paperwork: Any of these scenarios may be indicators of fraudulent activity.

Most computer crimes come under the jurisdiction of the local police and district attorney, although some crimes, such as those involving telephone fraud and export control violations, come under federal jurisdiction. If a discreet company investigation of an unusual business occurrence or security breach turns up the appearance of possible criminal activity, you should immediately contact your company attorney, local police department, and local district attorney's office. A willingness to report and vigorously prosecute cases of computer crime can help to prevent future fraud.

Appendix A

The following list provides names and phone numbers for agencies and organizations referred to in this publication. The second column provides a quick sketch of the areas of activity of each organization as it relates to our topic. If you have questions about any service or agency in the federal government, the Federal Information Center nearest you (see page 208) can provide information and help you to locate the appropriate agency.

The names, addresses, phone numbers, and office descriptions presented here have been checked thoroughly. However, because of changes that may take place after publication, some information may no longer be current. We regret any inconvenience this may cause.

These agencies and organizations	may provide answers and assistance in these areas
Audit Bureau of Circulations 900 North Meacham Road Schaumburg, IL. 60173 (708) 605-0909	Verify newspaper circulation figures.
Commodity Futures Trading Commission (CFTC) 2033 K Street, N.W. Washington, D.C. 20581 (202) 254-6387	Questions involving commodity futures trading and possible commodity futures fraud.

Regional CFTC Offices

Chicago
233 South Wacker Drive
Suite 4600
Chicago, IL 60606
(312) 353-5990

Kansas City
4900 Main Street
Suite 720
Kansas City, MO 64112
(816) 374-2994

Los Angeles
10850 Wilshire Boulevard
Suite 370
Los Angeles, CA 90024
(213) 209-6783

Minneapolis
510 Grain Exchange Building
Minneapolis, MN 55415
(612) 725-2025

New York
One World Trade Center
Suite 4747
New York, NY 10048
(212) 466-2061

Direct Selling Association 1776 K Street, N.W. Suite 600 Washington, D.C. 20006 (202) 293-5760	Questions involving door-to-door sales: verifying membership of companies involved in direct sales.

These agencies and organizations	may provide answers and assistance in these areas
Federal Bureau of Investigation United States Department of Justice Washington, D.C. 20535	All violations of federal law except those specifically assigned to other federal agencies.

The FBI's field offices are located in major cities throughout the U.S. and San Juan, Puerto Rico and resident agencies (suboffices) are maintained in smaller cities and towns in all parts of the country. The front page of most telephone directories lists the telephone number of the nearest FBI field office.

Federal Information Centers

Alabama
Birmingham, Mobile
(800) 366-2998

Alaska
Anchorage
(800) 729-8003

Arizona
Phoenix
(800) 359-3997

Arkansas
Little Rock
(800) 366-2998

California
Los Angeles, San Diego,
San Francisco, Santa Ana
(800) 726-4995

Sacramento
(916) 973-1695

Colorado
Colorado Springs,
Denver, Pueblo
(800) 359-3997

Connecticut
Hartford, New Haven
(800) 347-1997

Florida
Fort Lauderdale,
Jacksonville, Miami,
Orlando, St. Petersburg,
Tampa, West Palm Beach
(800) 347-1997

Georgia
Atlanta
(800) 347-1997

Hawaii
Honolulu
(800) 733-5996

Illinois
Chicago
(800) 366-2998

Indiana
Gary
(800) 366-2998

Indianapolis
(800) 347-1997

Iowa
All locations
(800) 735-8004

Kansas
All locations
(800) 735-8004

Kentucky
Louisville
(800) 347-1997

Louisiana
New Orleans
(800) 366-2998

Maryland
Baltimore
(800) 347-1997

Massachusetts
Boston
(800) 347-1997

Michigan
Detroit, Grand Rapids
(800) 347-1997

Minnesota
Minneapolis
(800) 366-2998

Missouri
St. Louis
(800) 366-2998
All other locations
(800) 735-8004

Nebraska
Omaha
(800) 366-2998
All other locations
(800) 735-8004

New Jersey
Newark, Trenton
(800) 347-1997

New Mexico
Albuquerque
(800) 359-3997

New York
Albany, Buffalo,
New York, Rochester,
Syracuse
(800) 347-1997

North Carolina
Charlotte
(800) 347-1997

Ohio
Akron, Cincinnati,
Cleveland, Columbus,
Dayton, Toledo
(800) 347-1997

Oklahoma
Oklahoma City, Tulsa
(800) 366-2998

Oregon
Portland
(800) 726-4995

Pennsylvania
Philadelphia, Pittsburgh
(800) 347-1997

Rhode Island
Providence
(800) 347-1997

Tennessee
Chattanooga
(800) 347-1997
Memphis, Nashville
(800) 366-2998

Texas
Austin, Dallas,
Forth Worth, Houston,
San Antonio
(800) 366-2998

Utah
Salt Lake City
(800) 359-3997

Virginia
Norfolk, Richmond,
Roanoke
(800) 347-1997

Washington
Seattle, Tacoma
(800) 726-4995

Wisconsin
Milwaukee
(800) 366-2998

| **These agencies and organizations** .... | **may provide answers and assistance in these areas** |

Federal Trade Commission (FTC)
6th & Pennsylvania Avenue, N.W.
Washington, D.C. 20580
(202) 326-2222

Questions involving possible false advertising and other deceptive business practices.

Regional FTC Offices

Atlanta
1718 Peachtree Street, N.W.
Suite 1000
Atlanta, GA 30367
(404) 347-4836

Dallas
100 N. Central Expressway
Suite 500
Dallas, TX 75201
(214) 767-5501

San Francisco
901 Market Street
Suite 570
San Francisco, CA 94103
(415) 744-7920

Boston
10 Causeway Street
Suite 1184
Boston, MA 02222
(617) 565-7240

Denver
1405 Curtis Street
Suite 2900
Denver, CO 80202
(303) 844-2271

Seattle
915 Second Avenue
2806 Federal Building
Seattle, WA 98174
(206) 553-4656

Chicago
55 East Monroe Street
Suite 1437
Chicago, IL 60603
(312) 353-4423

Los Angeles
11000 Wilshire Boulevard
Suite 13209
Los Angeles, CA 90024
(213) 209-7890

Cleveland
668 Euclid Avenue
Suite 520 A
Cleveland, OH 44114
(216) 522-4207

New York
150 William Street
Suite 1300
New York, NY 10038
(212) 264-1207

Internal Revenue Service
1111 Constitution N.W.
Washington, D.C. 20224
(202) 566-3272

Filing a complaint against a deceptive charitable soliciting organization.

International Anticounterfeiting Coalition, Inc.
818 Connecticut Avenue, N.W.
Suite 1200
Washington, D.C. 20006
(202) 223-5728

Advice and information regarding product counterfeiting. Membership is open to all companies, firms, and associations wishing to participate in efforts to eradicate product counterfeiting. Semiannual meetings and seminars are held for the interchange of information through panel discussions.

International Franchise Association
1350 New York Avenue, N.W.
Suite 900
Washington, D.C. 20005
(202) 628-8000

Information on franchising and franchisors.

International Trade Commission
Washington, D.C. 20436
500 E. Street, S.W.
(202) 205-1819

Details on procedures to follow in obtaining an exclusion order against foreign product counterfeiting.

National Association of Credit Card Merchants
217 N. Seacrest Blvd., Box 400
Boynton Beach, FL 33425
(407) 737-7500

Information on prevention techniques for credit card and check fraud.

National Office Machine Dealers Association
12411 Wornall Road
Kansas City, MO 64145
(816) 941-3100

Information on returning unordered office supplies.

These agencies and organizations	**may provide answers and assistance in these areas**

Securities and Exchange Commission (SEC)
Office of Consumer Affairs
Information Services
450 5th Street, N.W.
Washington, D.C. 20549
(202) 272-7440

Questions about securities dealings: verifying registration of securities brokers and their firms.

Regional SEC Offices

Atlanta
Suite 788
1375 Peachtree Street, N.E.
Atlanta, GA 30367
(404) 881-4768

Denver
Suite 700
410 Seventeenth Street
Denver, CO 80202
(303) 844-2071

New York
75 Park Place
14th Floor
New York, NY 10007
(212) 264-1614

Boston
90 Devonshire Street
Suite 700
Boston, MA 02109
(617) 223-9900

Fort Worth
8th Floor
411 West Seventh Street
Fort Worth, TX 76102
(817) 334-3821

Seattle
3040 Jackson Federal Bldg.
915 Second Avenue
Seattle, WA 98174
(206) 553-7990

Chicago
Room 1204
Everett McKinley Dirksen Bldg.
219 South Dearborn Street
Chicago, IL 60604
(312) 353-7390

Los Angeles
5757 Wilshire Boulevard
Suite 500 East
Los Angeles, CA 90036-3648
(213) 965-3998

Washington
Ballston Center Tower 3
4015 Wilson Boulevard
Arlington, VA 22203
(703) 235-3701

U.S. Commissioner of Patents and Trademarks
Washington, D.C. 20231
(703) 557-4357

Registering trademarks, obtaining a list of registered patent attorneys in a specific geographic area; obtaining patents.

U.S. Copyright Office
Library of Congress
Washington, D.C. 20559
(202) 479-0700

Registering copyrights.

U.S. Customs Service
Department of the Treasury
1301 Constitution Avenue, N.W.
Washington, D.C. 20229
(202) 566-8195

Recording registered trademarks and copyrights. Contact the IPR branch of the Customs Service for information concerning patent surveys – (202) 566-6956.

Chief Postal Inspector
Fraud Section
U.S. Postal Service
475 L'Enfant Plaza West,
S.W.
Washington, D.C. 20260
(202) 268-2000

Reporting violations of federal postal laws, including phony invoices, solicitations disguised as invoices, and any scheme that includes documents sent through the U.S. mail.

Appendix B

The Council of Better Business Bureaus is a business-supported nonprofit organization devoted to the protection of the consuming public and the vitality of the free enterprise system. Serving as the national headquarters for the local Better Business Bureaus, the Council promotes truth in advertising, resolves consumer/business disputes, develops industry standards for advertising and sales, and conducts consumer information programs.

Philanthropic Advisory Service, a division of the Council, monitors and reports on national soliciting organizations and conducts counseling and educational activities to aid both contributors and nonprofit groups.

COUNCIL OF BETTER
 BUSINESS BUREAUS, INC.
4200 Wilson Blvd.
Arlington, VA 22203
(703) 276-0100

PHILANTHROPIC ADVISORY SERVICE
Council of Better Business Bureaus, Inc.
4200 Wilson Blvd.
Arlington, VA 22203
(703) 276-0100

UNITED STATES BUREAUS

ALABAMA
BIRMINGHAM, AL 35205
 1214 South 20th Street
 P.O. Box 55268 (35255-5268)
 (205) 558-2222
DOTHAN, AL 36301
 118 Woodburn Street
 (205) 792-3804
HUNTSVILLE, AL 35801
 501 Church Street, N.W.
 P.O. Box 383 (35804)
 (205) 533-1640
MOBILE, AL 36602
 707 Van Antwerp Building
 (205) 433-5494,95
MONTGOMERY, AL 36104
 Union Bank Building,
 Commerce St.,
 Suite 810
 (205) 262-5606

ALASKA
ANCHORAGE, AK 99503
 4011 Arctic Blvd.
 Suite 206
 (907) 562-0704

ARIZONA
PHOENIX, AZ 85014
 4428 North 12th Street
 (602) 264-1721

TUCSON, AZ 85705
 50 W. Drachman St.,
 Suite 103
 Inq. (602) 622-7651
 Comp. (602) 622-7654

ARKANSAS
LITTLE ROCK, AR 72204
 1415 South University
 (501) 664-7274

CALIFORNIA
BAKERSFIELD, CA 93301-4882
 705 Eighteenth Street
 (805) 322-2074

COLTON, CA 92324-0522
 290 N. 10th St., Suite 206
 P.O. Box 970
 (714) 825-7280

CYPRESS, CA 90630
 6101 Ball Road, Suite 309
 Inq. & Comp.
 (714) 527-0680

FRESNO, CA 93705
 1398 W. Indianapolis
 (209) 222-8111

LOS ANGELES, CA 90020
 3400 West 6th St.,
 Suite 403
 (213) 251-9696

MONTEREY, CA 93940
 494 Alvarado St., Suite C
 (408) 372-3149

OAKLAND, CA 94612
 510 16th St., Ste. 550
 (510) 238-1000

SACRAMENTO, CA 95814
 400 S. Street
 (916) 443-6843

SAN DIEGO, CA 92108-1729
 3111 Camino del Rio, North,
 Suite 600
 (619) 521-5898

SAN FRANCISCO, CA 94105
33 New Montgomery St.
Tower
(415) 243-9999

SAN JOSE, CA 95125
1505 Meridian Ave., Suite C
(408) 978-8700

SAN MATEO, CA 94402
400 S. El Camino Real
(415) 696-1240

SANTA BARBARA, CA 93101
402 E Carrillo St., Suite C
(805) 963-8657

SANTA ROSA, CA 95401
300 B Street
(707) 577-0300

STOCKTON, CA 95202
1111 North Center Street
(209) 948-4880,81

COLORADO
**COLORADO SPRINGS,
CO 80933**
3022 North El Paso,
P.O. Box 7970 (80933)
(719) 636-1155

DENVER, CO 80222
1780 S. Bellaire, Suite 700
Inq. (303) 758-2100
Comp. (303) 758-2212

FORT COLLINS, CO 80525
1730 S. College Avenue,
Suite 303
(303) 484-1348

PUEBLO, CO 81003
119 W. 6th., Suite 203
(719) 542-6464

CONNECTICUT
FAIRFIELD, CT 06430
Fairfield Woods Plaza,
P.O. Box 1410
2345 Black Rock Turnpike
(203) 374-6161

**WALLINGFORD, CT
06492-4395**
100 S. Turnpike Rd.
Inq. (203) 269-2700
Comp. (203) 269-4457

DELAWARE
WILMINGTON, DE 19808
2055 Limestone Rd.,
Ste. 200
(302) 996-9200

DISTRICT OF COLUMBIA
1012 14th St. N.W.,
14th Floor
(202) 393-8000

FLORIDA
CLEARWATER, FL 34620
13770 - 58th St., North,
Suite 309
(813) 535-5522

FORT MYERS, FL 33901
2976-E Cleveland Ave.
(813) 334-7331
(813) 334-7152

JACKSONVILLE, FL 32216
3100 University Blvd.,
South,Suite 239
(904) 721-2288

MAITLAND, FL 32751-7147
2605 Maitland Center Pkwy.
(407) 660-9500

MIAMI, FL 33014-6709
16291 N.W. - 57th Ave.
Inq. (305) 625-0307
Comp. (305) 624-1302

**NEW PORT RICHEY,
FL 34652**
250 School Road,
Suite 11-W
(813) 842-5459

PENSACOLA, FL 32501
400 S. Alcaniz St.
(904) 433-6111

PORT ST. LUCIE, FL 34952
1950 Pt. St. Lucie Blvd.,
Suite 211
(407) 878-2010

TAMPA, FL 33607
1111 N. Westshore Blvd.,
Suite 207
Inq. & Comp.
(813) 875-6200

**WEST PALM BEACH, FL
33409-3408**
2247 Palm Bch. Lakes Blvd.,
Suite 211
(407) 686-2200

GEORGIA
ALBANY, GA 31707
1319-B Dawson Road
(912) 883-0744

ATLANTA,GA 30303
100 Edgewood Avenue,
Suite 1012
(404) 688-4910

AUGUSTA, GA 30901
P.O. Box 2085 (30903),
624 Ellis St., Suite 106
(404) 722-1574

COLUMBUS, GA 31901
8 13th Street,
P.O Box 2587 (31902)
(404) 324-0712,13

MACON, GA 31211
1765 Shurling Drive
(912) 742-7999

SAVANNAH, GA 31416-0956
6606 Abercorn Street,
Suite 108-C
(912) 354-7521

HAWAII
HONOLULU, HI 96814
1600 Kapiolani Blvd.,
Suite 714
(808) 942-2355

IDAHO
BOISE,ID 83702
1333 West Jefferson
(208) 342-4649

IDAHO FALLS, ID 83402
1547 South Blvd.
(208) 523-9754

TWIN FALLS, ID 83301
705 Blue Lakes Blvd., N.
(208) 736-3971

ILLINOIS
CHICAGO, IL 60606
211 West Wacker Drive
Inq. (312) 444-1188
Comp. (312) 346-3313

PEORIA, IL 61615
3024 West Lake
(309) 688-3741

ROCKFORD, IL 61104
810 E. State St., 3rd Fl.
(815) 963-2222

INDIANA
ELKHART, IN 46514
722 W. Bristol St.,
Suite H-2,
P.O. Box 405 (46515)
(219) 262-8996

EVANSVILLE, IN 47715
4004 Morgan Ave.,
Suite 201
(812) 473-0202

FORT WAYNE, IN 46802
1203 Webster Street
(219) 423-4433

GARY, IN 46408
4231 Cleveland Street
(219) 980-1511

INDIANAPOLIS, IN 46204
Victoria Centre,
22 E. Washington Street,
Suite 310
(317) 637-0197

SOUTH BEND, IN 46637
52303 Emmons Road,
Suite 9
(219) 277-9121

IOWA
BETTENDORF, IA 52722
852 Middle Rd., Suite 290
(319) 355-6344

DES MOINES, IA 50309
615 Insurance Exchange
Building
(515) 243-8137

SIOUX CITY, IA 51101
318 Badgerow Building
(712) 252-4501

KANSAS

TOPEKA,KS 66607
501 Jefferson, Suite 24
(913) 232-0454

WICHITA, KS 67202
300 Kaufman Bldg
(316) 263-3146

KENTUCKY

LEXINGTON, KY 40507
311 W. Short Street
(606) 259-1008

LOUISVILLE, KY 40203
844 S. Fourth Street
(502) 583-6546

LOUISIANA

ALEXANDRIA, LA 71301
1605 Murray St., Suite 117
(318) 473-4494

BATON ROUGE, LA 70806
2055 Wooddale Blvd.
(504) 926-3010

HOUMA, LA 70360
501 E. Main Street
(504) 868-3456

LAFAYETTE, LA 70506
100 Huggins Rd.,
P.O. Box 30297 (70593)
(318) 981-3497

LAKE CHARLES, LA 70602
3941-L Ryan Street,
P.O. Box 7314 (70606)
(318) 433-1633

MONROE, LA 71201-7380
141 De Siard Street,
Suite 808
(318) 387-4600

NEW ORLEANS, LA 70130
1539 Jackson Avenue
(504) 581-6222

SHREVEPORT, LA 71107
1401 North Market Street
(318) 221-8352

MAINE

PORTLAND, ME 04103
812 Stevens Avenue
(207) 878-2715

MARYLAND

BALTIMORE, MD 21211-3215
2100 Huntingdon Avenue
(301) 347-3990

MASSACHUSETTS

BOSTON, MA 02116-4404
20 Park Plaza, Suite 820
Inq. (617) 426-9000

SPRINGFIELD, MA 01103
293 Bridge Street,
Suite 320
(413) 734-3114

WORCESTER, MA 01608
32 Franklin Street,
P.O. Box 379 (01601)
(508) 755-2548

MICHIGAN

GRAND RAPIDS, MI 49503
620 Trust Building
(616) 774-8236

SOUTHFIELD, MI 48076-7751
30555 Southfield Road
Suite 200
Inq. (313) 644-1012
Comp. (313) 644-9136

MINNESOTA

**MINNEAPOLIS-
ST. PAUL, MN 55116**
2706 Gannon Road
(612) 699-1111

MISSISSIPPI

JACKSON, MS 39206-3088
460 Briarwood Drive,
Suite 340
(601) 956-8282

MISSOURI

KANSAS CITY, MO 64106
306 E.12th Street,
Suite 1024
(816) 421-7800

ST. LOUIS, MO 63110
5100 Oakland, Suite 200
Inq. (314) 531-3300

SPRINGFIELD, MO 65806
205 Park Central East,
Suite 509,
P.O. Box 4331 GS
(417) 862-9231

NEBRASKA

LINCOLN, NE 68504
719 North 48th Street
(402) 467-5261

OMAHA, NE 68102
417 Farnam Street
(402) 346-3033

NEVADA

LAS VEGAS, NV 89104-1515
1022 E. Sahara Avenue
(702) 735-6900
(702) 735-1969

RENO, NV 89515
991 Bible Way,
P.O. Box 21269
(702) 322-0657

NEW HAMPSHIRE

CONCORD, NH 03301
410 South Main Street
(603) 224-1991

NEW JERSEY

NEWARK, NJ 07102
494 Broad Street
(201) 642-INFO

PARAMUS, NJ 07652
2 Forest Avenue
(201) 845-4044

PARSIPPANY, NJ 07054
1300 A Route #46 West
(201) 334-5990

TOMS RIVER, NJ 08753
1721 Route 37 East
(201) 270-5577

TRENTON, NJ 08690
1700 Whitehorse,
Hamilton Square, Suite D-5
Mercer County
(201) 588-0808
Monmouth County
(201) 588-0808
Middlesex, Somerset
and Hunderton Counties
(201) 588-0808

WESTMONT, NJ 08108-0303
16 Maple Avenue
P.O. Box 303
(609) 854-8467

NEW MEXICO

ALBUQUERQUE, NM 87109
4600-A Montgomery N.E.,
Suite 200
(505) 884-0500

FARMINGTON, NM 87401
308 North Locke
(505) 326-6501

LAS CRUCES, NM 88005
2407 W. Picacho, Ste. B-2
(505) 524-3130

NEW YORK

BUFFALO, NY 14202
346 Delaware Avenue
(716) 856-7180

FARMINGDALE, NY
(Long Island) 11735
266 Main Street
(516) 420-0500

NEW YORK, NY 10010
257 Park Avenue, South
(212) 533-7500

ROCHESTER, NY 14604
1122 Sibley Tower
(716) 546-6776

SYRACUSE, NY 13202
100 University Building
(315) 479-6635

**WAPPINGER FALLS,
NY 2590**
1211-Route #9
(914) 297-6550
WHITE PLAINS, NY 10603
30 Glenn Street
(914) 428-1230,31

NORTH CAROLINA
ASHEVILLE, NC 28801
801 BB&T Building
(704) 253-2392
CHARLOTTE, NC 28204
1130 East 3rd St.,
Suite 400
(704) 332-7151
GREENSBORO, NC 27410
3608 West Friendly Ave.
(919) 852-4240,41,42
HICKORY, NC 28613
3305-10 16th Ave.,
SE #303
(704) 464-0372
RALEIGH, NC 27604
3120 Poplarwood Ct.,
Suite 101
(919) 872-9240
**WINSTON-SALEM,
NC 27103**
2110 Cloverdale Ave.,
Suite 2-B
(919) 725-8348

OHIO
AKRON, OH 44303-2111
222 W. Market Street
(216) 253-4590
CANTON, OH 44703
1434 Cleveland Ave,, N.W.
(216) 454-9401
CINCINNATI, OH 45202
898 Walnut Street
(513) 421-3015
CLEVELAND, OH 44115
2217 East 9th Street
(216) 241-7678
COLUMBUS, OH 43215
1335 Dublin St., #30A
(614) 486-6336
DAYTON, OH 45402
40 West Fourth St.,
Suite 1250
(513) 222-5825
LIMA, OH 45802
P.O. Box 269
(419) 223-7010
MANSFIELD, OH 44902
130 W. Second St.,
P.O. Box 1706 (44901)
(419) 522-1700
TOLEDO, OH 43604-1055
425Jefferson Avenue,
Suite 909
(419) 241-6276
WOOSTER, OH 44691
345 N. Market
(216) 263-6444

YOUNGSTOWN, OH 44501
311 Mahoning Bank Bldg.,
P.O. Box 1495
(216) 744-3111

OKLAHOMA
OKLAHOMA CITY, OK 73102
17 S. Dewey
Inq. (405) 239-6081
Inq. (405) 239-6860
Comp. (405) 239-6083
TULSA, OK 74136-3327
6711 South Yale, Suite 230
(918) 492-1266

OREGON
PORTLAND, OR 97205
610 S.W. Alder Street,
Suite 615
(503) 226-3981

PENNSYLVANIA
BETHLEHEM, PA 18018
528 North New Street
(215) 866-8780
LANCASTER, PA 17602
6 Capital Court
1-800/220-8032
Toll Free, York Co.
Resident
(717) 846-2700
PHILADELPHIA, PA 19103
1930 Chestnut St.,
P.O. Box 2297
(215) 496-1000
PITTSBURGH, PA 15222
610 Smithfield Street
(412) 456-2700
SCRANTON, PA 18503
601 Connell Building,
6th Floor
P.O. Box 993 (18501)
(717) 342-9129

PUERTO RICO
SAN JUAN, PR 00936-3488
P.O. Box 363488
(809) 756-5400

RHODE ISLAND
WARWICK, RI 02887-1300
Bureau Park, Box 1300
Inq. (401) 785-1212
Comp. (401) 785-1213

SOUTH CAROLINA
COLUMBIA, SC 29201
1830 Bull Street
(803) 254-2525
GREENVILLE, SC 29601
113 Mills Ave.
(803) 242-5052
MYRTLE BEACH, SC 29577
1310-G Azalea
(803) 497-8667

TENNESSEE
BLOUNTVILLE, TN 37617
P.O. Box 1176 TCAS
(615) 323-6311
CHATTANOOGA, TN 37402
1010 Market Street,
Suite 200
(615) 266-6144
KNOXVILLE, TN 37915
900 East Hill Ave.,
Suite 165
(615) 522-2552
MEMPHIS, TN 38115
3792 South Mendenhall
P.O. Box 750704
(38175-0704)
(901) 795-8771
NASHVILLE, TN 37239
One Commerce Place,
Suite 1830
(615) 254-5872

TEXAS
ABILENE, TX 79605
3300 S. 14th Street,
Suite 307
(915) 691-1533
AMARILLO, TX 79101
1000 South Polk
(806) 358-6222
AUSTIN, TX 78701
221 W. 6th St.
Suiite 450
(512) 476-1616
BEAUMONT, TX 77704
P.O. Box 2988
476 Oakland Ave. (77701)
(409) 835-5348
BRYAN, TX 77803
202 Varisco Building
(409) 823-8148,49
CORPUS CHRISTI, TX 78411
4535 S. Padre Island Drive
(512) 854-2892
DALLAS, TX 75201
2001 Bryan Street,
Suite 850
(214)220-2000
EL PASO, TX 79903
1910 East Yandell
(915) 545-1212
FORT WORTH, TX 76102
512 Main Street, #807
(817) 332-7585
HOUSTON, TX 77008
2707 North Loop West,
Suite 900
(713) 868-9500
1-800/669-1430
LUBBOCK, TX 97408
1015 15th Street,
P.O. Box 1178
(806) 763-0459
MIDLAND, TX 79711
10100 County Rd.,
118 West
(915) 563-1880

SAN ANGELO, TX 76904
3121 Executive Dr.,
P.O. Box 3366
(76902-3366)
(915) 949-2989
SAN ANTONIO, TX 78217
1800 Northeast Loop 410,
Suite 400
(512) 828-9441
TYLER, TX 75701
3502-D South Broadway
P.O. Box 6652
(75711-6652)
(214)581-5704
WACO, TX 76710
6801 Sanger Avenue
Suite 125
P.O. Box 7203
(76714-7203)
(817) 772-7530
WESLACO, TX 78596
116 West Fifth,
P.O. Box 69
(512) 968-3678
WICHITA FALLS, TX 76301
1106 Brook Avenue
(817) 723-5526

UTAH
SALT LAKE CITY, UT 84115
1588 South Main Street
(801) 487-4656

VIRGINIA
FREDERICKSBURG, VA 22407
4022-B Plank Road
(703) 786-8397
NORFOLK, VA 23509
3608 Tidewater Drive
(804) 627-5651
(804) 851-9101
(Peninsula area)
RICHMOND, VA 23219
701 East Franklin,
Suite 712
(804) 648-0016
ROANOKE, VA 24011-1301
31 West Campbell Ave.
(703) 342-3455

WASHINGTON
KENNEWICK, WA 99336
127 W. Canal Drive
(509) 582-0222
SEATTLE, WA 98121
2200 Sixth Avenue,
828 Denny Building
(206) 448-8888
SPOKANE, WA 99204
S. 176 Stevens
(509) 747-1155
TACOMA, WA 98401
1101 Fawcett Ave.,
#222 (98402),
P.O. Box 1274
(206) 383-5561

YAKIMA, WA 98907
P.O. Box 1584
424 Washington Mutual
Bldg. (98901)
(509) 248-1326

WISCONSIN
MILWAUKEE, WI 53203
740 North Plankinton Ave.
(414) 273-1600

INTERNATIONAL BUREAUS

NATIONAL HEADQUARTERS FOR CANADIAN BUREAUS
CONCORD, ONTARIO
L4K 2Z5
2180 Steeles Avenue West
Suite 219
(416) 699-1248

ALBERTA
CALGARY, ALBERTA
T2H 2H8
7330 Fisher Street, S.E.,
Suite 350
(403) 258-2920
EDMONTON, ALBERTA
T5N 2L9
9707 - 110th Street
(403)482-2341
Red Deer, Alberta
(403) 343-3280

BRITISH COLUMBIA
VANCOUVER, BC V6B 2M1
788 Beatty Street,
Suite 404
(604) 682-2711
VICTORIA, BC V8W 1V7
201-1005 Langley Street
(604) 386-6348

MANITOBA
WINNIPEG, MANITOBA
R3B 2K3
365 Hargrave Street,
Room 204
(204) 943-1486

NEWFOUNDLAND
ST. JOHN'S, NEWFOUNDLAND A1E 2B6
360 Topsail Road,
P.O. Box 516 (A1C 5K4)
(709) 364-2222

NOVA SCOTIA
HALIFAX, NOVA SCOTIA
B3J 2A4
P.O. Box 2124,
1731 Barrington Street
Inq. (902) 422-6581
Comp. (902) 422-6582

ONTARIO
HAMILTON, ONTARIO
L8P 4V9
50 Bay Street, South
(416) 526-1111
KITCHENER, ONTARIO
N2G 2P7
220 Charles Street, East
(519) 579-3080
LONDON, ONTARIO
N6A 3C2
304 York Street
P.O. Box 2153 (N6A 4E3)
(519) 673-3222
OTTAWA, ONTARIO
K1P 5N2
71 Bank Street, 6th Floor
(613) 237-4856
ST. CATHERINES, ONTARIO
L2R 3H6
11-101 King Street
(416) 687-6686
TORONTO, ONTARIO
M6P 4C7
One St. John's Rd.,
Suite 501
(416) 766-5744
WINDSOR, ONTARIO
N9A 5K6
500 Riverside Drive West
(519) 258-7222

QUEBEC
MONTREAL, QUEBEC
H3A 1V4
2055 Peel Street, Suite 460
(514) 286-9281
QUEBEC CITY, PQ G1R 1K2
475 Rue Richelieu
(418) 523-2555

SASKATCHEWAN
REGINA, SASKATCHEWAN, S4N 6H4
1601 McAra Street
(306) 352-7601

Glossary of Terms

Advance Fee Loan Scheme. See LOAN BROKER SCHEME.

Advertising Solicitation Scheme. A scam in which a bogus "advertising salesperson" cons businesses into placing ads in nonexistent or worthless publications, often at inflated rates. May include the issuing of SOLICITATIONS IN THE GUISE OF INVOICES.

"Bank-financed" Precious Metal Scheme. A common tele-marketing ploy in which the operator promises huge profits from an investment in gold or silver. In this complicated scam, the con artist arranges for bank financing of part of the precious metals purchase, then soaks the victim with fees that wipe out most or all of his or her investment.

Bankruptcy Fraud. Any of a variety of schemes in which a business – whether a legitimate or bogus firm – utilizes the federal bankruptcy laws to defraud creditors.

Blind Pool Penny Stock Scam. A telemarketing scam in which the victim is talked into investing "blind" in a penny stock company without any specified plan for making profits. Typically, the promoter manipulates the stock price and sells out when it reaches its peak, deflating the price and leaving the investor with shares in a valueless stock.

Boiler Rooms. Low-rent offices crammed with salespeople who call hundreds of prospects each day in the operation of OFFICE SUPPLY SCHEMES, telemarketing investment scams, and other telemarketing fraud.

Booster Box. One of the devices used by professional shoplifters, the booster box is a large box with a hinged end, top, or bottom that sometimes is gift wrapped to avoid detection.

Break-out Artist. A dishonest employee who hides inside an office or plant in order to steal goods after closing hours.

Bust-out. A variation of BANKRUPTCY FRAUD in which the operator of a business secretly closes up operations and moves on, leaving behind a trail of disgruntled creditors.

Check Kiting. A form of embezzlement in which a person takes advantage of the "float" period – the time between when a company deposits a check and its bank collects the funds – to withdraw ever-increasing amounts from the corporate account.

Civil Demand Letter. Permitted in several states, civil demand letters are sent by retailers to accused juvenile shoplifters to deter repeat violations by asking the offender to share some of the costs of store security.

Computer Virus. Coded instructions hidden in a computer program that enable the programmer to alter and/or destroy data. Sophisticated viruses can lie dormant or spread silently for weeks or months, waiting for a trigger, such as a specific date, before springing to life.

Container Switch. In this crime practiced on retail businesses, the thief replaces the contents of a ticketed container with higher-priced merchandise or hides goods inside another bag or box.

Credit Laundering. An arrangement in which a merchant agrees to deposit another merchant's bankcard drafts in its own credit card merchant account in return for a commission or fee. The processing merchant can suffer financial losses and termination of its merchant account and, if fraud is involved, criminal prosecution.

Currency Switch. A form of counterfeiting in which money is tampered with so the bills appear to be of a higher denomination. See also RAISED NOTE.

Damage Claim Artist. A con artist who feigns injury in an office or retail establishment, threatens to sue, and then "settles for" an out-of-court payment.

Digital Signature. As related to computer security, this is a code tacked onto a software program to enable the purchaser to tell if the program has been tampered with.

Directory Advertising Scheme. A form of ADVERTISING SOLICITATION SCHEME in which businesses are misled into paying for ad space in nonexistent or worthless directories, such as business or telex directories. See also FAX DIRECTORY SCHEME.

Draft Laundering. See CREDIT LAUNDERING.

Dummy Supplier. A phony company invented by an embezzler who also fabricates records of purchases and then collects on the payments made to the nonexistent vendor.

Fair Market Value. The price at which property would change hands between a willing and knowledgeable buyer and seller.

Fax Directory Scheme. A twist on the SOLICITATIONS IN THE GUISE OF INVOICES SCHEME in which a targeted business receives legitimate-looking invoices for phantom listings in nonexistent telefax number directories.

Foreign Bank Investment Scam. A telemarketing scheme in which the operator promises unusually high profits from investments in overseas banks. The con artist commonly pockets the "investments" and vanishes.

Ink Tags. Plastic antitheft tags that, when improperly removed from merchandise, release indelible ink onto both the garment and the shoplifter.

Intellectual Property Rights. The exclusive ownership of an original product of the thought processes. As defined by the federal government, intellectual property rights include patents, trademarks, copyrights, and MASK WORKS.

Knockoffs. Unlike counterfeit products, which are designed to look as much like the original as possible, knockoffs are near-copies with a brand name slightly different from the original or labeled with a word such as "replaces" in small type before the forged brand name logo.

Lapping. A form of embezzlement that involves the temporary withholding of receipts, such as payments of accounts receivable. Lapping is a complicated scheme that usually starts with a small amount but can run into thousands of dollars before it is detected.

Loan Broker Scheme. An unethical takeoff on the legitimate loan broker business, in which a broker helps businesses or consumers locate loan sources. In a loan broker scheme, a con artist charges an "advance fee," or deposit, without intending either to provide the promised service or refund the fee.

Mask Work. A new type of intellectual property protected by the Semiconductor Chip Protection Act of 1984. A mask work is defined by the federal government as the design of an electrical circuit, the pattern of which is transferred and fixed in a semiconductor chip during the manufacturing process.

Multilevel Marketing. A legitimate form of retailing in which independent distributors sell the products or services of a marketing company and, in most cases, receive commissions or bonuses for recruiting and managing other salespeople. Compare with PYRAMID SCHEME.

Nonregistered Sales. A form of embezzlement in which a cashier fails to ring a sale in the cash register and then steals the cash that should have been deposited.

Office Supply Scheme. A swindle carried out by a PAPER PIRATE or WATS-LINE HUSTLER in which businesses are deceived into purchasing off brands of office supplies, such as photocopier paper or toner, typewriter ribbons, and cleaning compounds.

Paper Flrm. A fictitious insurance company created to defraud businesses that exists only in the form of its worthless paper policies.

Paper Pirate. A con artist who specializes in OFFICE SUPPLY SCHEMES. Paper pirates frequently carry out their operations by phone, using carefully scripted pitches to ensure that their unethical dealings remain within the pale of the law. Also known as toner-phoners.

Payroll Fraud. A form of embezzlement in which an employee collects on checks issued to nonemployees whose names have been added to the company payroll.

PBX Fraud. A relatively new form of telephone fraud in which thieves obtain the access numbers to a company's PBX, or corporate switchboard, and place hundreds of costly calls that are charged to the company's phone bill.

Phony Invoice Scheme. A scheme that involves the issuing of invoices or past-due notices for undelivered goods and services. Most involve an initial phone contact in which the con artist gathers information that permits the mailing of a legitimate-looking but fraudulent invoice.

Pyramid Scheme. An illegal variation of the MULTILEVEL MARKETING system in which the intent of the promoters is to recruit new promoters rather than to sell a product or service.

Quick-change Artist. A fast-talking con artist who, through a rapid and confusing exchange of currency, tricks store cashiers into handing over more change than is deserved.

Raised Note. Paper currency altered in an attempt to increase its face value. One common method is to glue numerals from high-denomination bills onto the corners of lower denominations.

Security Thread. A new feature added to U.S. currency to help deter counterfeiting. The polyester thread is embedded in the paper on all bills except the one-dollar denomination.

Short Packaging. A form of cargo theft in which merchandise placed on a truck for shipment is pilfered at the loading dock without the driver's knowledge. When the driver discovers the theft at the delivery point, he usually is held responsible for the shortage.

Solicitations in the Guise of Invoices Scheme. A variation on the PHONY INVOICE SCHEME in which solicitations for the purchase of goods or services are designed to look like legitimate invoices for goods or services ordered and received.

Spectrum Analyzer. A bug detector that searches the air for listening devices transmitting over radio frequencies.

Tax Deductible. An organization that is eligible to receive donations that may be deducted from the donor's federal income tax.

Tax Exempt. An organization that is not required to pay taxes. Compare with TAX DEDUCTIBLE.

Teleblackmail. A twist on the OFFICE SUPPLY SCHEME in which victims who place orders are "rewarded" with free gifts; the scam operator later threatens to go to the victim's boss about the acceptance of the gift unless the employee places additional orders or approves fraudulent invoices.

Toner-phoner. See PAPER PIRATE.

Trusted System. As related to computer security, a trusted system is a computer security measure that limits user access to specified files and, in some cases, limits the functions the user can perform.

Voltage Detector. A "tap alert" that warns of the presence of an invasive, or on-the-line, phone tap when it detects deviations from the phone line's normal voltage.

WATS-Line Hustler. A term coined by law enforcement officials for OFFICE SUPPLY SCHEME operators who use long-distance telephone lines, including WATS-lines, to carry out their scams.

Index

Numbers in *italics* represent charts and graphs.

Advance fee loan schemes, 51-58
Advertising solicitation schemes, 29-31, 43-44, 84, 88-89, 216
Affidavit, sample, 36
American Association of Fund Raising Counsel, 38
American Bankers Association, 126
American Insurance Association, 188
Art print scam, 82
Audit Bureau of Circulations, 33, 151-52

Bad checks, *See* Check, fraud
"Bank-financed" precious metals schemes, 82, 216
Bankruptcy fraud, 59-63, 216
Better Business Bureau, 16, 23, 25, 32, 35, 38, 45, 48, 53, 58, 62, 78, 91, 152
Blind pool penny stock scams, 83, 216
Boiler rooms, 90, 216. *See also* Office supply schemes
Booster box, 216
Break-out artist, 217
Bribery, 181-86
Business opportunity schemes, 65-78
Business-to-business dealings, 183-86
Bust-out, 217

Cargo theft, 152-58
Cashiers, crimes practiced on, 103-13
"Chain letter" schemes. *See* Pyramid schemes
Chargebacks, credit card fraud and, 128
Charity solicitation schemes, 37-49
Check
    fraud, 133-45, *135*
    kiting, 176-77, 217
Civil demand letters, 124, 217
Commercial counterfeiting. *See* Product counterfeiting
Computer crime, 162-64, 195-206, 217
Conference Board, 164
Container switches, 111-12, 217
Copycat government documents, 34

Copyrights, 99
Council of Better Business Bureaus, 13-14
    Philanthropic Advisory Service, 13, 39, 44, 45, 48
Counterfeiting
    coupons, 151
    credit cards, 129-31
    currency, 106-10
    desktop forgery, 200
    investigations, 98
    products, 95-102
    trends, *106*
Couponing, 148-49
Coupon(s), *148, 149*
    fraud, 147-52
Credit card
    fraud, 125-32
    laundering, 128, 217
    usage, 126-27, *126, 127*
Crime prevention. *See* Protecting business against
Currency switches, 105-6, 217

Damage claim artist, 190, 217
Data tampering, 198
Delivery vehicle theft, 157-58
Desktop forgery, 200
Digital signature, 217
Directory advertising schemes, 31-32, 218
    See also Advertising solicitation schemes; Fax directory schemes
Draft laundering, 217, 218
Dummy suppliers, 177, 218

Electronic espionage, 161-62
Embezzlement, 171-80
Employee
    leaks of information, 160-61
    theft, 171-80
Encryption systems for computers, 203
Exchange fraud, 112-13
Expense account fraud, 177
Fair market value, 218

Fax directory schemes, 31, 218. *See also* Solicitations disguised as invoices
Federal Bureau of Investigation (FBI), 12, 13, 63, 145, 158, 206
Federal Trade Commission (FTC), 20-22, 24, 25, 66, 75, 78, 80, 81, 90-91, 126
Foreign bank investment scams, 83, 218
Foreign industrial espionage, 163
Franchising, *69, 70, 71*
  fraud, 67
Fraud
  bankruptcy, 61-62
  check, 136-42
  coupon, 150-52
  credit card, 129-31
  exchange, 112-13
  expense account, 177
  franchising, 67
  insurance, 187-94
  invention marketing, 75-76
  land development, 72
  loan broker, 51-58, 219
  PBX, 85-86, 89-90, 219
  refund, 112-13

Government-business dealings, 183-85

If you are victimized. *See* Recourses
Industrial espionage, 159-67
Information crimes, 159-67
Ink tags, 218
Insurance fraud, 187-94
Intellectual property rights, 99, 100, 218
Internal Revenue Service (IRS), 40-42, 48, 206
International Anticounterfeiting Coalition(IACC), 96, 100-1
International Trade Commission (ITC), 96, 101
Invention marketing fraud, 72-73
Investment schemes, 65-78, 81-86

Kickbacks, 181-86
Knockoffs, 96-97. *See also* Counterfeiting

Land development fraud, 72
Lapping, 176, 218
Loading dock crime, 156-57
Loan broker frauds, 51-58, 219

Mail-order business scams, 68
Manipulation of input data, 198
Mask works, 99, 219
Medical insurance schemes, 191
Merchandise offered by charities, 45-46
Misuse of computer time, 198
Multilevel marketing schemes, 69-72, 219

National Advisory Commission on Criminal Justice Standards and Goals, 182-83, 184-86
National Association of Attorneys General, 90-91
National Association of Credit Card Merchants, 126
National Association of Independent Insurers, 192
National Cargo Security Council, 154
National Futures Association, 91
National Institute of Justice, 15
National Office Machine Dealers Association, 24
National Office Products Association, 12, 20, 21
Newspaper industry guidelines for coupons, 151-52
900-number ripoffs, 84-85, 89
Nonregistered sales, 175-76, 219
North American Securities Administrators Association, 80
Notice of returned check, sample, *144*

Office supply schemes, 12, 19-25, 219
Overshipments, 154-55

"Paper firms," 189, 219
Paper pirates, 19-25, 219
Patents, 99
Payoffs, 181-86
Payroll fraud, 177, 219
PBX fraud, 85-86, 89-90, 219
Philanthropy, contributions made to, and recipients of, *49. See also* Charity
Phony advertising solicitations, 29-31
Phony invoice schemes, 27-36, 220
Pilferage, 171-180
Police, 25, 35, 48, 78, 91, 113, 145, 158
Precious metals schemes, 82, 216
Price tag switches, 110-11
Product counterfeiting, 12, 95-102
Profiles
  credit card criminals, 127-29
  shoplifters, 116-17
Programming crimes, 197-98
Protecting business against
  "advance fee" schemes, 54-58
  bankruptcy fraud, 61-62
  bribery, 184-86
  business opportunity schemes, 74-77
  cargo theft, 154-58
  charitable solicitation schemes, 38-48
  check fraud, 136-42
  computer crime, 201-5
  coupon fraud, 150-52
  credit card fraud, 129-31
  crimes practiced on cashiers, 104-13
  embezzlement, 175-80

franchising and sales opportunity schemes, 75
industrial espionage, 164-66
insurance fraud, 189-94
invention marketing fraud, 75-76
kickbacks, 184-86
loan broker frauds, 54-58
office supply schemes, 22-23
"paper pirates," 22-23
payoffs, 184-86
phony invoice schemes, 32-35
pilferage, 172-75
shoplifting, 117-22
telemarketing crimes, 86-90
Pyramid schemes, 69-72, 220

Quick change artists, 104-5, 220

Raised note, 220
Recourses (if you are victimized)
"advance fee" schemes, 58
bribery, 186
business opportunity schemes, 77-78
cargo theft, 158
charitable solicitation schemes, 48
check fraud, 142-46
computer crime, 205-6
coupon fraud, 152
credit card fraud, 131-32
crimes practiced on cashiers, 113
embezzlement, 180
industrial espionage, 166-67
insurance fraud, 194
intellectual property counterfeiting, 101
kickbacks, 186
loan broker frauds, 58
office supply schemes, 23-25
"paper pirates," 23-25
payoffs, 186
phony invoice schemes, 36
pilferage, 180
product counterfeiting, 101
shoplifting, 122-23
telemarketing investment scams, 90-91
Refund fraud, 112-13

Securities and commodity futures investments, 83
Security software, 204
Security thread, 220
Shoplifting, 115-24
Short packaging, 156-57, 220
Small Business Administration (SBA), 12, 56-57, 122-23, 172, 175, 178

Solicitations disguised as invoices, 29-32, 220. See also Phony invoice schemes
Spectrum analyzer, 165, 220
State attorney general, 24, 25, 48, 152

"Tap alert." See Voltage detector
Tax deductions, 40-42, 43-44, 220
Tax exempt groups, 40, 220
Teleblackmail, 86, 221. See also Office supply schemes
Telemarketing crimes, 19-25, 79-91, 128
Theft
cargo, 152-58
computer output, 199
corporate electronic, 159-67
by data transfer, 199
employee, 171-80
prevention, 178-80
shoplifting, 115-24
retail, 12
"Toner phoners." See Office supply schemes
Trademarks, 99
Trade names, 99
Trusted system, 204, 221

U.S. Census Bureau, 196
U.S. Chamber of Commerce, 183, 184-86
U.S. currency, 107-10
counterfeiting, 106-10
U.S. Customs Service, 101
U.S. Department of Commerce, 96
U.S. Department of Justice, 206
U.S. Patent Office, 75-76
U.S. Postal Service, 24, 28, 35, 48, 58, 78, 91, 152
regulations, 24, 33-34
U.S. Secret Service, 113, 145, 206
Unauthorized shipments, 154-55
Unordered merchandise, 24-25, 47
UPC codes, price tag switching, and, 111

Vending machine fraud, 68
Victimized, if you are. See Recourses
Voltage detector, 165, 221

"WATS-line hustlers," 20-22, 25, 221
See also Office supply schemes
White-collar crimes, 12-13, 13
Work-at-home schemes, 73

Yellow pages bills, phony, 31